BUT GOD

A Supernatural Journey

BEHRUZ DAROGA

WESTBOW
PRESS®
A DIVISION OF THOMAS NELSON
& ZONDERVAN

WestBow Press books may be ordered through booksellers or by contacting:

WestBow Press
A Division of Thomas Nelson & Zondervan
1663 Liberty Drive
Bloomington, IN 47403
www.westbowpress.com
844-714-3454

Because of the dynamic nature of the Internet, any web addresses or links contained in this book may have changed since publication and may no longer be valid. The views expressed in this work are solely those of the author and do not necessarily reflect the views of the publisher, and the publisher hereby disclaims any responsibility for them.

Any people depicted in stock imagery provided by Getty Images are models, and such images are being used for illustrative purposes only. Certain stock imagery © Getty Images.

Scripture taken from the King James Version of the Bible.

Scripture taken from the NEW AMERICAN STANDARD BIBLE®, Copyright © 1960,1962,1963,1968,1971,1972,1973,1975,1977,1995 by The Lockman Foundation. Used by permission. www.Lockman.org

Scripture taken from the New King James Version® Copyright © 1982 by Thomas Nelson. Used by permission. All rights reserved.

ISBN: 978-1-6642-1054-7 (sc)
ISBN: 978-1-6642-1053-0 (hc)
ISBN: 978-1-6642-1055-4 (e)

Library of Congress Control Number: 2020921304

Print information available on the last page.

WestBow Press rev. date: 12/01/2020

CONTENTS

Preface ix

Acknowledgments xi

Chapter 1   Beginning 1

Chapter 2   Growing in faith.. 9

Chapter 3   Protection..17

Chapter 4   Crucified...25

Chapter 5   Unspeakable 35

Chapter 6   Trial Conduct..41

Chapter 7   Healing 49

Chapter 8   Marriage..60

Chapter 9   The Rapture...66

Chapter 10 Preparation 75

Chapter 11 The End 82

Epilogue...87

I dedicate this book to the following people:

To the late Konrad Sonderregar, who led me to Christ and mentored me in the Bible and personal evangelism.

To my wife, Vijeya, for being my faithful and constant partner throughout the ups and downs of married life for thirty-five years.

To Catch the Fire church for the amazing teaching, fellowship, and spiritual growth in the Holy Spirit. It is where I received the teaching and anointing for healing.

To Pastor Steve Long, who played a big part in mentoring me in the ministry of the Holy Spirit when I was part of his connect group.

To Pastor John Bootsma for his warm friendship and teaching while I was part of his connect group.

To my two sons, Daniel and Joshua, who I hope will be inspired by this book to press in for all that God has for them and also for all the prophesies expressed to them.

And to all those through whom I have felt the sea of love in various and diverse ways and at sundry times when I was going through my trials.

Let us hear the conclusion of the whole matter: Fear God, and keep His commandments: for this is the whole duty of man. For God shall bring every work into judgement, with every secret thing, whether it be good, or whether it be evil.

—Ecclesiastes 12:13–14 (KJV)

PREFACE

Really? This is all every person has to do? Fear God and keep His commandments? However, if you do, you will be targeted by the world, the devil, and the flesh. But the Lord will step in. This will set the stage for a series of events that will be an incredible rollercoaster the likes of which you never imagined. "Things which eye has not seen and ear has not heard, and which have not entered the heart of man, all that God has prepared for those who love Him" (1 Cor. 2:9 NASB).

Great. All I do is come to God, obey Him, and keep His commandments and everything will be hunky-dory. Not quite. That is not what the verse says. That is human thinking. The verse is talking about a roller coaster ride with God, the maker of heaven and earth, the omnipotent, omnipresence, and omniscient God. "For as the heavens are higher than the earth, so are My ways higher than your ways, and My thoughts than your thoughts." (Isa. 55:9 NASB).

"You need to write a book," someone remarked to me as I was enjoying a cup of coffee in the church cafe. I was amused. That was the farthest thing from my mind. I did not see myself as an author. I was unknown. Years later, another person said the same thing. I had the same reaction. Years later, a prominent prophet said she saw me writing a book. This time I gave it a thought, but write about what? Most of what I knew I had learned from other authors. Then years later, another prophet said the same thing.

This time I gave it serious thought, and this time I actually inquired about it to the Lord. I should have done that the first time!

The Lord said, "You have a history with me. Write about that." Oh crumbs! I never kept a journal! But I discovered that God stories are unforgettable. This book is my history and roller-coaster ride with God. It is full of stories that illustrate the truths in the Bible. The stories are grouped into chapters that undergird particular truths in scripture. For this reason, the book is not a chronology of my life.

My parents were not Christians, but on their death beds, they came to Christ. However, they left their house to an occultist charity even though I was the only surviving child of three. They gave half the cash they had to another occultist church and to my aunties. I received the other half, which amounted to 15 percent of the estate. However, the Lord said, "I am your inheritance." I did not understand that, apart from the knowledge of my reward being in heaven. As I was writing this book, I realized it was my legacy from the Lord. It is all about Him.

ACKNOWLEDGMENTS

I acknowledge the Holy Spirit for bringing to my remembrance all the miraculous events described in this book, even when I did not journal. I also acknowledge Him for the inspiration I received even while writing this book.

I acknowledge WestBow Press for their editing and publication services and Stephen Alagaratnam for proofreading the manuscript and for his helpful suggestions.

Honour your father and mother [which is the first commandment with a promise], so that it may be well with you, and that you may live long on the earth.

—Ephesians 6:2–3 (NASB)

CHAPTER 1

―――― ◈◆◈ ――――

BEGINNING

MOTHER

"Pray to God to heal you by naming these names of God [in my former religion Zoroastrian] and Jesus Christ," my mother said in the middle of the night as I lay at death's door at the age of five. But that was not God's plan for my life. My mother did not know Jesus Christ as God or Savior but included the name, as He was the only one in any religion to have a reputation for healing. I had been very ill for six months with every childhood sickness, one after another— measles, chicken pox, even smallpox, mumps, malaria, and arthritis after being bedridden for so long. I also had typhoid.

But this last sickness would just not respond to treatment. I was running a very high fever, and the whole family, including aunts and uncles, were frantically trying to control it with ice bottles, soaking towels, etc. Acetaminophen was not around at that time. I was administered penicillin and sulphur drugs, but to no avail. Later, I discovered that the prolonged use of these drugs rendered my body unresponsive to penicillin, and I was allergic to sulphur drugs. This allergy later proved to be life-threatening as well.

Shortly after I started praying that prayer every day, my parents made the most important decision of their lives concerning me.

They changed doctors. The new doctor correctly diagnosed my disease as typhoid and treated me for it. I recovered. I had the distinct impression that I had a guardian angel over me all my life. It would be fifty-three years before I was seriously ill again. However, God would save my life twelve more times between then and now. This recovery was also the first of numerous miracles in my life. And later, the Holy Spirit would partner with me to perform hundreds of miraculous healings in peoples' lives.

Years after I recovered, I would lead my mother at the age of ninety-one, on her death bed and on Mother's Day, to Jesus Christ. Before that, I would experience—and still am experiencing—the most tumultuous, wild, crazy, and exhilarating lifelong ride with the Holy Spirit. "Eye hath not seen, nor ear heard, neither have entered into the heart of man, the things which God hath prepared for them that love Him" (1 Cor.2:9 KJV).

NARROW ESCAPE

I heard a long crunching noise, and the pole came crashing down onto one of the children I was playing with. Next thing I knew, he was lying on the ground, dead. This was the second time God saved my life.

My parents had immigrated to England but did not include us children, as my mother needed prolonged treatment there. They planned to send for us when they were settled and had bought a house for the family. During this time, my sister, brother, and I were under the care of my aunt and uncle in Mumbai at the Parsi apartment complex, which had the playground where the accident happened. That evening, my aunt would not let me go play until I had finished the school assignment of memorizing "All Creatures Great and Small." After a while, I went out and played with the other children around a large pole with ropes hanging from the top. We would hold the ropes and run and swing around the pole. But this time, the pole snapped and landed on another boy.

Reflecting on this, I wonder if the outcome of that accident would have been different if I had gone to play earlier. That discipline to study placed me in good stead later in my academic career.

Apart from this experience, my memories of growing up in India until the age of thirteen are happy ones. I rode hired bicycles, flew kites, went roller-skating, played with sticks and stones, and played hide-and-seek. We also attended the fire temple, where we worshipped God through the burning of incense. The teaching boiled down to this: good words, good thoughts, and good deeds.

ENGLAND

The cold air slammed into my face. This was my first experience of cold weather. My parents called my sister, brother, and me over to England, and we found ourselves under the care of our uncle on our way. We had a stop in Frankfurt, Germany, and had stepped out of the plane and onto the tarmac. It was the winter of 1960. This first flight was fascinating to me as an adventurous thirteen-year-old. Little did I know, years later I would begin experiencing the wildest ride ever imagined with the Holy Spirit.

BUT GOD

"You will be attending Loxford Secondary School, and your brother will be attending Barking Abbey Grammar School," my father said to me. We had completed taking the eleven-plus tests that separated students into two streams: grammar and secondary. The grammar stream was taught all the science and advanced mathematics subjects that were omitted in the secondary stream. I was disappointed. It meant I would not be able to pursue a professional career. But God had other plans.

At the school I attended, biology, applied and advanced mathematics, and French were not in the curriculum, so my father enrolled me in correspondence courses for these extracurricular subjects. In addition, I attended evening classes at the school for the subjects taught in my class. He also hired a private tutor to teach me French. I cannot say this workload was easy. The discipline of not playing until I had finished my work had put me in good stead now. I went to London to sit for the GCE O-Level exams in the extracurricular subjects. I passed with good grades. I was then eligible to enrol in the grammar school.

GRAMMAR SCHOOL

"Behruz, you can do anything you want to do if you put your mind to it," my biology teacher said to me. I had failed some subjects in the GCE A-Level and chose to repeat the year at the grammar school. I had slacked in my discipline as I went out drinking every night with my friends. But that comment renewed my discipline, and I got good grades in my science subjects. And her words stuck with me throughout my life.

"Do not become an engineer; there is too much discrimination and politics in this field. Become a doctor. Doctors, especially from India, are well respected," my father told me. I had wanted to become an engineer like my father, especially since I was good at math, physics, and science. My applications to medical school were unsuccessful. I was among the leading edge of the baby boomers, competition was fierce, and spending that extra year at A-Level had not helped.

In any case, it was exceptional for someone to go straight from A-Level to medical school. One stepping-stone was to earn a bachelor of science degree. So I tried to enrol in universities but was unsuccessful again. I was accepted to a college of advanced technology for an honors degree but only managed to receive an ordinary degree. That put an end to my hopes of a medical career. Among the baby boomers, degrees came two for a penny. But God again had different plans for me. Years later, God partnered with me to perform hundreds of miraculous healings. *But God* would very much be the experience of my life. Not only in the sense that God had different plans than me, but also in the sense of God rescuing me from dangers, being my advocate in trials, and stilling the storms I experienced.

CONVERSION

"Do you have a Bible at home?" the evangelist asked in a European accent. I was distributing pamphlets for a photography competition at the 1972 Dagenham town show to promote the Barking Photographic Society, of which I was a member. As I turned, I saw he was unlike any other person I had met. He had a pile of Bibles in different languages and any number of scriptural tracts. I replied no. My prayers, since the age of five, in the name of the five names, had been answered up to this time. I had a firm belief in God, so when I was offered a free Holy Bible, I accepted it, promised to read it, and said I would stay in touch. We exchanged contact information. His name was Konrad Sonderregar, and he became a big part of my life in England.

We met every week to discuss what I had been reading. He understood that I was not asking questions to challenge the Bible but to find answers. As I read the Bible I knew it was the Word of God; I felt it was very authoritative.

One day, I asked him, "If God wanted us to love Him of our own free will, why would He be angry if we chose not to?"

He replied, "If you were married, you would want your wife to love you of her own free will."

Just as I was leaving, we had the following chat at the door.

Konrad asked, "Do you believe Jesus Christ died for you?"

"Yes."

"Do you believe He is the Son of God?"

"Yes."

5

"Do you believe He rose from the dead and is seated at the right hand God the Father?"

"Yes."

"Do you take Jesus as your Lord and Savior?"

"Yes."

Then he led me through the sinner's prayer and proclaimed, "You are saved."

"GIVE UP TV."

That's what the Lord said to me. I thought it was probably a good idea. So I spent the time devouring the Bible and read it from cover to cover in one year. As the saying goes, "Read the Bible and pray every day, and you will grow and grow." I also read books by Kathryn Kuhlman and Rees Howells, as well as the periodical *Herald of His Coming* and the book *Late Great Planet Earth*. I read about Charles Finney, Evan Roberts, and others who God partnered with to bring revivals. It was during this time that I surrendered unconditionally to the Holy Spirit, three years after my conversion. The teachings of Reverend Cardy at the Highway Evangelical Church on 1 Corinthians discipled me in the Christian life. I have read numerous other books all through my life that have had a huge impact on me, which I will mention later. It was also during this time that I developed a zeal for God, which I will also describe later.

SUICIDAL

Academic studies prepare you for a career; biblical studies, with the knowledge going to your heart not just your head, prepare you for the storms of life. Such was the case for me when I experienced several storms that hit me like a "Minnesota blizzard" (in the words of Max Lucado), to the extent that I was suicidal. However, the Holy Spirit came flooding in, and I was comforted. "When the enemy shall come, in like a flood the Spirit of the Lord shall lift up a standard against him" (Isa.59:19 KJV). This was the third time God saved my life. I will expand on this more later on. To further strengthen my faith through these storms, sweet Jesus (in the words of Heidi Baker) let me experience—not just read about—His miracles for three years before the storms hit.

Ask, and it shall be given to you; seek, and you will find; knock, and it will be opened to you.

—Matthew 7:7 (NASB)

CHAPTER 2

GROWING IN FAITH

LOW ODDS HUNTING

I prayed, "Lord, I need a pair of shoes with leather tops and leather soles that will last longer than the cheap shoes with rubber soles that I can only afford. But I cannot afford more than £5. I had been wearing old shoes with worn-out rubber soles that had holes in them. I would stuff wads of newspaper into the shoes when the weather was wet, which was more often than not. The Lord said to go shopping.

Off I went to Main Street, and I started window-shopping. I expected the Lord to have the shoes displayed in the window. However, after shopping the length and breadth of the street, there was no joy. I was about to turn back when the Lord said to go farther. I did, and lo and behold, there was one more shop farther down. There in the window, I saw them: leather tops, leather soles, size 8, £5. My size, my shoes, my price! Is Jesus alive or what? I talk to Him as if He is right beside me.

BEFORE YOU ASK

On another occasion, I found a pile of almost new shirts cleaned and neatly folded right outside my home where garbage is left for pickup.

They were my size. I had been wearing worn old shirts my parents had bought for me years ago. I had not even prayed for shirts! God is so good!

CRUISE

"Lord, you have forty-five minutes, Lord you have thirty minutes, Lord you have fifteen minutes," I said. I love traveling and had come across an opportunity to go on a three-day cruise for a ridiculously low fare of £29, all-inclusive. This was out of this world even for prices forty-six years ago. I could not persuade any of my friends to come with me. So I went alone.

It was 1973, one year after I became a Christian. The ship was sailing from Portsmouth, England, and I was in London. I left with plenty of time to get to Portsmouth station, which was only a short taxi ride away from the port. I arrived at Portsmouth one hour before the ship was due to sail. As I ventured outside, my heart sank. There was a long, long queue for the taxies. I thought it was just as well that I had arrived one hour before the ship left the dock.

But the queue was moving at a snail's pace. For some reason, taxies were not getting through to the station. Hence, I started reminding God of how much time He had left. After being silent all the time that I was reminding Him, the Lord finally answered, "Are you trying to tell me how much time I have got left?" I answered, "It's like this. You said I could go, but it seems I am not going to make it to the ship in time." Jesus replied, "I am able to do exceeding abundantly above all you can ask or think" (Eph.3:20 KJV).

So I was thinking, *He said I could go. I am not going to make it to the ship by departure time. He can do exceedingly above all I can ask or think.* So I said, "You are going to hold up the whole ship just for me?" The Lord replied, "That's right."

It was about an hour and a half past the departure time when I finally got into a taxi. The couple behind me asked if they could come with me, as they were on the same cruise, and offered the taxi fare. When we reached the pier, to my amazement, the ship was still docked. I climbed the stairs, and no sooner than I registered, the ship blew the departure whistle. I asked the bursar why the ship did not sail at the scheduled time, and he replied, "We heard that there was an accident and the resulting traffic jam prevented the taxies from coming through to the station. So we waited for the three of you." *Wow.* The power and goodness of the Lord to hold up the ship just for me! And to pay my taxi fare!

FINDING KONRAD

"Where is Konrad's letter?" I asked my parents.

I had kept in touch with Konrad, but he had moved. My parents were not at all pleased that I had met him. They feared he was one of those cultic leaders who drew children away from their parents. They kept all his letters from me. There was no social media or internet, for that matter. I sometimes think the Lord invented mobile phones and internet just for me. So I had no clue where he moved to or any contact information. So I turned to God.

"Go start looking for him in the neighbourhood at his last known address," the Lord said. I started going around the streets near his last address even though that made no sense. Isn't God amazing? I soon saw him walking down the street where I happened to be!

These "acts of the Holy Spirit" in my life, from the first at age five, would prepare me for the "fiery darts of the wicked" in the storms I would experience later. "As an eagle stirs up its nest, hovers over its young, spreading out its wings, taking them up, carrying them on its wings, so the Lord alone led him and there was no foreign god with him" (Deut.32:11–12 NKJV). An eagle teaches her young to fly by taking off with her young on her wings, soaring high, and then dropping them off in the air. As they tumble to the ground, she catches all of them one by one in midair and soars high again to repeat the process until the young learn to fly. The Lord was teaching me to trust Him and fly with Him. I have continued to experience victories right up to present day through the ups and downs of my Christian life. Through these, the Lord has shown me the spiritual principles (that I will describe later) of the Christian life and how "God causes all things to work together for good to those who love God, to those who are called according to His purpose" (Rom.8:28 NASB). Not only that, but the Lord also showed me what it would take for the church to be protected and provided for during the tribulation.

WALT DISNEY WORLD

"I was supposed to meet my friend at the car in the parking lot, but now the spot has changed. Would you be able to give a message over the broadcast system for John Emms to meet me at a certain place?" I asked as a last resort.

"Cannot do that," the woman replied.

I was in a panic. Vijeya (my wife) and I had invited John and Margaret Emms, our pastors from England, over to Canada for a holiday at Walt Disney World in 1987. They were exceptionally good to my wife (how I met her is an amazing story I will describe later) when we were in England, and we wanted to show our appreciation. However, during the day, Margaret felt she was slowing us down with the problem with her hip. So John and Margaret decided to explore on their own, leaving Vijeya and I to do the same. We agreed to meet at the car after the fireworks at the end of the day. The day was very hot, and Vijeya could not take the sun very well. After struggling through the day, I finally agreed to take her back to the apartment where we were staying. This meant, of course, that John and Margaret would not be able to meet us at the car because when I came back, I was parked in a different spot! In Disney World's parking lot! If you know the place, you know what a huge problem that is. There was no way to communicate with them about what had happened. This was before mobile phones and internet. Hence, my request to the public broadcaster.

I was in a pickle. I vainly tried to do what I did to find Konrad, but I soon realized the futility of it. So I said, "Lord, it is impossible for me to find them now as I am moving and they are moving. I will stay opposite the Magic Castle during and after the fireworks. You will just have to bring them to me at that time." Can you imagine how I felt when, after the fireworks, John and Margaret passed within an arm's reach of me? Can you imagine what that did to my faith? They were so blown away with my story that they related it to churches when they were preaching.

Return of the Prodigal

"I am looking for Deborah," I said to the receptionist at the hotel.

"Just take a seat in the conference. She should be there," she replied.

I neglected to tell her that I didn't know what Deborah looked like. *Never mind*, I thought. *I will ask inside.*

My wife had phoned me at work about Deborah, who had come to her door about a product she was selling and asked if my wife would be interested in being an agent. She answered that she will check with me. My wife phoned me and said that Deborah would be at the conference in the hotel near my place of work.

So I was sitting, waiting for the conference to begin, and vainly trying to look at badges of people passing by. The Lord said, "Why don't you do what you did at Walt Disney World?" I replied, "There I knew what the people looked like. I do not know what Deborah looks like." What the Lord said next surprised me: "How do you want me to tell you this is Deborah?" I thought for a moment and replied You will just have to impress it on my mind."

I noticed a lady pass me and sit behind me. "This is Deborah," the Lord said. *No, it cannot be*, I thought, as it was so incredible. "Debbie," a voice called out behind me. *What?* I thought. *It cannot be.* Another voice called out, "Debbie." Finally the Lord said, "You asked me to impress upon you. I am impressing upon you that this is

Deborah." At this, I turned around and asked her if she was Deborah. She answered yes! We decided against becoming agents, as it was multiple-level marketing. But after we told her how I knew she was Deborah, she quit as an agent and went back to the Lord. Perhaps that was the whole point of this exercise.

CANADA DAY, 150TH ANNIVERSARY

"D" was hoping to deliver her baby on the 150th anniversary of Canada Day (which was the following day), but the delivery date was two weeks after that, her father told me. So on the way to Kingston, I put this to the Lord. On a stopover, I heard the Lord say she would deliver the baby on Canada Day. So over coffee, I told the group that the Lord said we should pray for that. We did. The mother was a bit incredulous, since the contractions had not commenced and it was already 4:00 p.m. on June 30. I kept telling the mother that I'd had a breakthrough, but she humored me.

"Keep praying, keep praying," she said excitedly on Canada Day. "The contractions started last night," but D had not told me. Sure enough, the baby was delivered early in the evening on Canada Day. It is the Father's good pleasure to give us our wants as well as our needs in the same way it is my good pleasure to give my children, say, a bicycle and to see them riding it.

HARRODS

The women in London were afraid to go out at night or walk through parks or open the door to strangers. A killer and rapist was stalking the streets of London, killing women. The police had failed to make an arrest in over three months. Several women were killed. Now why would anyone at Harrods, where I was working, look at me suspiciously? So I took this to the Lord and proclaimed to my coworkers that the killer would be caught within two weeks. He was.

Bang. Evidently a bomb was detonated outside Harrods and two police officers were killed. Sometime later, the buyer casually remarked to me that the police wondered why the terrorists did not plant the bomb inside Harrods.

I told her I recalled a customer who had an old Harrods card. The cards were replaced a long time ago, but the old cards were still valid, as there were no expiration dates on them. He had asked what would happen if there were a bomb threat. I should have referred him to management. But hey, he had a Harrods card, so I had assured the customer that Harrods had a very good system to locate any bombs inside the store.

I narrated this to the buyer. Two weeks later, the buyer informed me that they had caught the guy. It was the same customer. They were able to trace the old card, as there were very few of them in circulation, and with the date and time of the purchase he made, they were able to ID the person. His phone was wiretapped, and that was how he was caught.

This was an era when terrorist activities were rampant, and the Lord said, "You have come to the kingdom for such a time as this" (Est.4:14 NKJV). Since then, I have continued to pray for the enforcement agencies whenever and wherever I hear in the news about the police seeking the public's help. Several cases have been solved, even several cold cases from fifty years ago.

Why am I narrating this? It may not be significant, but my last name means "chief inspector of police!"

He who dwells in the shelter of the Most High
will abide in the shadow of the Almighty.

—Psalm 91:1 (NASB)

CHAPTER 3

PROTECTION

At Cliff's Edge

"Lord, help!" I cried out as I found myself accidentally on the edge of a cliff with no way up or down.

In 1962, two years after I immigrated to England, I went on a school-organized walking tour of the Lake District in England. The bus dropped us at the base of a mountain and picked us up again to take us to our next youth hostel and mountain. Halfway through that trip, I suffered a sprained ankle and missed half the trip. I said to myself, "I am coming back."

Fourteen years later, I ventured out on a walking tour of the Lake District on my own, having unsuccessfully tried to persuade my friends to join me. Armed with an ordinance survey map and compass, I set out. One day, as I was walking along the top of a hill, I noticed the trail was heading west and making a loop back to a short distance farther down from where I was standing. I could see the destination ahead of me as well. *Why not just go straight down and cut across the other side of the loop?* I thought. The slope seemed gentle enough.

That was very deceptive. The next thing I knew, I was on the edge of a cliff. It was only later, when I studied the map closely, that

I realized I had come down some crags, very easy to come down but impossible to get back up again, that ended with a precipitous drop. That was why the trail made such a wide detour. Where were mobile phones when I needed them? Ah yes, I remember it well. They were not invented yet.

So there I was, perched three hundred feet above the ground on a narrow ledge, alone, with no one knowing my whereabouts. I did not have faith for the Lord to bear me up if I jumped. The Lord said, "Look to your right." About three hundred yards along the ledge, barely eighteen inches wide, I noticed a stone quarry that came up to about twenty feet below the ledge. I had a backpack as well. Facing the cliff, trying to grip whatever I could with my hands, I inched my way toward the quarry. I finally arrived at a spot where I felt I could jump onto the stones. I prayed there would not be a stone avalanche. Taking a deep breath, I jumped. I slid about three hundred feet down the hill, but no avalanche. Praise the Lord. This was the fourth time the Lord saved my life. I almost wet my pants but not quite. But I did want to go to the washroom badly.

Quicksand

Where can I relieve myself? I thought to myself the same afternoon on the same trail. It ran through a forest not one hundred yards from the road. I noticed a clump of trees farther away to the left of the trail. The ground was flat with no steep drops, but disaster still struck! No sooner did I take my first step off the trail than I found myself in quicksand. The ground was covered with leaves, so I did not notice the mud.

I was sinking. I remembered reading in *Reader's Digest* how to survive and come through quicksand. The strategy did not work. Perhaps it had something to do with my backpack that was still on my back! I did not want to dump my backpack. It had everything, including my ID. It was only at this point that I cried out to the Lord. I noticed a clump of grass within arm's reach. I grabbed it and tugged at it to make sure it was firm. It was, and I was able to pull myself out of the quicksand. This was the fifth time the Lord saved my life.

But I was covered from head to toe with mud! I opened the backpack, and to my relief, the clothes were not covered in mud as well. So right there, about one hundred yards from the road, I stripped down completely naked, wiped myself with towels, dressed in clean clothes, and relieved myself there without risking going farther from the road. But I still looked a sight when I registered at the hostel. I don't think the receptionist believed my story.

DIVERTICULITIS ABSCESS

I was in agony. I was in England visiting my father and had developed diarrhoea. So I took some tablets, but that had a limited effect. I took one tablet of a stronger medicine, but that produced severe constipation. I had invited some friends from my days in England out to dinner. That evening, I was in agony. I could not keep any food down. I was due to fly back home to Canada the following day, so I did not want to go to the emergency room. At home in Canada, I tried to drink some orange juice. I could not keep that down. The only thing I could take was water.

I went to our family doctor, who ordered blood tests. She called back and told me to report immediately to the emergency room. I was diagnosed with diverticulitis abscess. I later discovered that the walls of two adjacent folds of my colon were fused, and that supported the wall of the colon, which was very thin as a result of the abscess. If the wall was breached, my chances of survival were very slim. This was the sixth time the Lord saved my life.

ALLERGY

However, the diagnostic procedure itself almost proved fatal. "Did you ever have asthma?" the doctor asked. I remembered having a bout of it for a short time a long time ago. It had been a long time since I needed inhalers. So I replied no. The doctor explained that patients who had asthma were prone to be allergic to the CT dye used in the CAT scan. The result could be suffocation. I replied that I had not suffered from asthma.

Sure enough, when the dye was injected, I was suffocating. I could not breathe. The nurse could see I was in distress. I again cried out to the Lord, repenting my denial, and I took authority over this reaction in Jesus' name. I was able to breathe again. This was the seventh time the Lord saved my life.

STRESS TEST

"Your chart shows there is hidden high blood pressure that occurs infrequently," my doctor said. She ordered a stress test that involved using a treadmill. When I felt I could not do any more, I told the technician I'd had enough. However, I had forgotten that I had to quit when I felt I could not go on for another two minutes. The technician needed to read my blood pressure before he could stop the treadmill. I prayed I would be able to go for another two minutes. Later, the doctor said I had asked for the treadmill to stop just in time, as the consequences could have been dire if I had gone on any longer. They did have an emergency team on standby. This was the eighth time the Lord saved my life.

HEPATIC VEIN

"What is happening?" Vijeya, my wife, exclaimed. I was shaking violently in the middle of the night. I had no explanation. I took two antihistamine tablets, as I thought it might be an allergic reaction to something. After a while, it subsided.

However, two days later, I was shaking violently again, this time during the day. I didn't think it was God, as I felt afraid. So I went to the doctor, who ordered blood tests. After reviewing the results, she told me to go immediately to the emergency room. The results showed all blood levels were abnormal. I went to emergency, and Pastor Steve Long visited me there. CAT scans showed my liver was almost completely shot. I was asked repeatedly by several medical staff if I had been abroad. I repeatedly answered no. Steve brought some doughnuts and Tim Horton's coffee for me. A few minutes later, I was shaking violently again, in emergency, right in front of the doctor. My blood pressure was dangerously high.

Finally, an infectious disease specialist was called in. She looked at the CAT scans carefully and explained that these were not the typical Hepatitis scans that the medical staff were suspecting. Hence, their questioning whether I had been abroad. Upon closer examination, she noticed the infection was stemming from my small intestine. The problem was diverticulitis again, and the infection had spread from the intestine to the liver, resulting in all blood levels being abnormal. The blocked vein would be the cause of my high blood pressure and shaking. This would be the ninth time the Lord saved my life.

"We will have to operate," the nurse explained. "The antibiotics are ineffective."

"No," I replied anxiously. "You need to give me Vitamin C with the antibiotics for them to be effective. I want to talk to the doctor."

That the doctor came to see me was remarkable enough. I explained, "Some patients require vitamin C with antibiotics and some do not. I require vitamin C. Research shows this. Please look it up."

That the doctor looked it up and prescribed vitamin C was a miracle. The same antibiotics were effective. After this, she had a big teleconference with the medical profession. I could not help thinking back to the time I could not get admission to a medical school. But God. Later she asked me, "How do you know so much about drugs?"

I heard about the vitamin C in the news but just replied, "I work in the pharmaceutical industry."

SALINE DRIP

Not again, I thought. I was back in the hospital with diverticulitis for the third time. This time, the diagnosis was made sooner and I was given antibiotics with vitamin C. However, one of my very young visitors was inquisitive and fiddled with the knob of the saline drip. I anxiously cautioned him not to touch anything. He tried to turn the knob back to where it was but could not. I didn't think too much of it. Next thing I knew, after the visitors had left, I felt very faint. The saline drip that was supposed to last for eight hours lasted barely one hour. The visitor had opened the drip up.

Fortunately, I had asked my wife to bring me some Gatorade. This was to reduce the swelling in my body caused by the constant saline drip. The osmotic pressure of the Gatorade from the sugar and salts would draw the water from under the skin and into the bloodstream and out through the kidneys.

When the drip was opened up, the water must have got into my brain. I barely had enough time to drink a lot of Gatorade before I passed out and put my life in God's hands. I recovered a couple of hours later. I was still groggy but made my way to the washroom even though I was a bit unsteady. The nurse on duty was scolded, but it had not been her fault.

It could very well have been the tenth time my God saved my life.

JOSHUA

"Where is Joshua?" Vijeya cried out frantically.

While on vacation at a waterfront resort in Canada, our real estate agent called us to say he had an offer to buy our rental apartment. We needed to negotiate and sign the papers. As we were five hours out of town, we agreed to do this over the phone. However, this meant using a fax machine to fax the papers back and forth with our signatures for each offer and counteroffer. We had to this at reception, since that was the only place with a fax machine.

Well, we could not leave Daniel, age six, and Joshua, age four, at the unit alone, so we had to take them with us to reception. It was getting dark. We told our sons to stay in the reception area and not to go out. They were restless after a while and asked if they could stay outside the glass doors where we would still be able to keep an eye on them. We agreed.

Not two minutes later, Vijeya turned around and saw our sons were missing. She rushed outside and saw Daniel standing near the edge of the lake. She could not see Joshua!

She rushed back to reception and cried out to me, "Joshua's in the water!" I rushed to the shore to see his head bobbing in and out of the water. I could not swim either. I tried vainly to reach my son from the edge, but he was just out of reach.

"Jump!" a voice shouted from about three hundred yards away from the pier. He was staying at the unit next to us. So I jumped. If it meant my life for his, so be it. To my immense relief, the water only came to my chest! I could not see the depth of the water because it was dark. I grabbed him and gave him to Vijeya. However, I could not get on top of the shore, and my neighbor, who had run over to help, had to fish me out!

We could not imagine life without either of our sons. In a manner of speaking, our lives were also saved.

Be of good cheer! It is I; do not be afraid.

—Matthew 14:27 (NKJV)

Before I formed you in the womb I knew you, and before you were born I consecrated you; I have appointed you a prophet to the nations.

—Jeremiah 1:5 (NASB)

CHAPTER 4

CRUCIFIED

ZEAL

What I was watching made me sick. Christians and priests were the butt of jokes by different comedians on TV. I grew up in England in the 1960s during the sexual revolution, the permissive society, and the "age of Aquarius." Up until the conversion, I had made the same jokes. I had not yet gotten the memo about what Jesus did for me. But now those jokes made me sick. *I am not going to do anything to bring dishonor to God*, I said to myself and told God I wanted to glorify His name. I did not realize it at that time, but thinking about it now, that was very much like Peter when he told Jesus that he would never forsake Him. And very much like Peter, I was in a pickle. Again! And not in the same way as when I went on a cruise or went to Walt Disney World.

Indeed, in the culture I was in, I longed to see God work again as He did with Kathryn Kuhlman, Rees Howells, Charles Finney, Charles Wesley, Evan Roberts, and others. A Baptist church I attended for a brief time held an evening prayer meeting for revival along the lines of 2 Chronicles 7:14. I confessed my sins, as "revival has to start with you," but there was no revival in sight.

I prayed for revival and for healing for the patients in the hospital every day on my commute on the London Underground to the research institute I was working in, and in midweek church prayer meetings at another church I attended after I left the Baptist church. But still there was no revival in sight. Once when we were singing the song "Here I Am to Worship," I was struck by the words, "I'll never know what it cost to see my sin upon the cross." I asked the Lord, "What did it cost?" That may have been a mistake. Or maybe not. He soon showed me! I was crucified. "Unless a grain of wheat falls into the earth and dies, it remains alone; but if it dies, it bears much fruit" (John 12:24 NASB). But the Lord showed me that that experience was like a pinprick compared to what He experienced. I was blissfully ignorant of the cost of revival. "It takes a crucified man to preach a crucified savior." (Periodical Herald of His Coming. Not in circulation now).

I soon found myself the butt of jokes, and covertly at that. In God's providence, this did not happen before I experienced God in the events described previously. Those acts of the Holy Spirit were an anchor for my faith during this time.

DOUBLE MEANING

After the Sunday evening service, a few members met just for a time of worship and fellowship. This evening, most of the church members were laughing their heads off. Anything anyone said had a double meaning. A few members were not laughing but were instead looking at me sympathetically and painfully to see what was happening to me. This was my only solace. This happened every week for six months.

During this time, I often had panic attacks. I remember telling the Lord that I wanted to glorify His name. This was not glorifying His name. This was not what I signed up for.

During this time, I prayed through the psalms (Psalm 6, 7, 10, 17, 22, 25, 31, 32, 35, 38, 41–43, 51, 54–57, 69–71, 77, 86, 88, 94, 102, 109, 120, 130, 140–143). These psalms were for sin and affliction, persecution, expressing trust in God's goodness, mercy, power, majesty, and glory and in the psalmists' integrity, gratitude, adoration, "Be of good cheer," the Lord said. "It is I. Be not afraid." Finally, the Lord said to pray for them and forgive them.

Raised from the Dead

Once after the Sunday morning service, I was invited to the prayer room. During prayer, we had word that one of the members had dropped dead. I was in disbelief. This was confirmed by one of the members who was a nurse.. We prayed for him, and he came back to life. This was told to the prayer meeting, but I was in even more disbelief. Since then, I have tried several times to pray for the dead, but nothing. I realized that "the Lord restored the fortunes of Job when he prayed for his friends" (Job 42:10 NASB). Later, the Lord revealed to me that in a one-in-a-million chance, a telephone line was crossed, someone overheard a conversation, and the truth was made known, and I was vindicated. Mostly vindicated. Apparently, my food was adulterated with Andriol, or a salt of testosterone. Why?

The Lord revealed that the life I was leading was convicting the other tenants in the building and that someone was being manipulative and set me up so that they could accuse me. The Lord allowed them to succeed. I was crucified.

When I was traveling on a bus, still praying, suddenly there was a manifest presence of the Holy Spirit. I did not recognize it as such at that time. In fact, I asked my parents, "What does it mean when someone is blushing?" Years later (in a meeting where Bobby Connor spoke, in Canada), I realized that there was nothing in me to glorify the Lord's name but that God could partner with me to glorify His name. God would say, "Pray for them," and people would stop blushing. This continued for years wherever I went. It was only many years later that the Lord said He was judging them as they judged me. Shortly after the manifest presence of the Holy Spirit, I moved back to my parents and joined another church.

DROUGHT

There was a severe drought in England. England is known for wet weather most of the time. Jokes about the wet English weather run rampant. I used to crack them. A drought in England! The media called it the finger of God. Spain, which normally has scarce rain, had deluge of rain. The holiness church I was attending at that time held a prayer meeting one evening midweek. I decided to attend. The Lord said, "If you are going to pray for rain, take an umbrella with you!"

"SWEET JESUS" (HEIDI BAKER)

I felt utterly foolish walking along the street with an umbrella during a drought. The very few people who attended the meeting raised their eyebrows at the risk I was taking. I had already made myself enough of a fool when I was crucified, and here I was risking being a fool again. What if it did not rain after the meeting and I did not need the umbrella? Well, after the meeting, when we left there was no rain!

As I lay in bed, complaining to God, suddenly there was a *boom, crash, bang, wallop*. "Praise the Lord! Thank you, Jesus!" I exclaimed. "But you could have done this during the meeting" I complained. The Lord explained that if the rains had come during the meeting, only a few people would have known I had arrived with an umbrella. They would have given thanks and glorified God. But that's all. However, after the meeting the news of what I had done spread through telephone calls (still no social media or smart phones). Now God was glorified in the sight of the whole country. Isn't Jesus sweet, even when I was complaining! The following morning, the news media declared the drought was broken with a vengeance! To my astonishment, the Lord said something that blew my mind. He was giving me the anointing of Elijah!

BIBLE COLLEGE

Soon after, the Lord called me into ministry. I put this to the church. They felt that since I was a research laboratory assistant, I could serve in their medical laboratory in India. I resigned from my job and attended the Bible college in Manchester, England. The manifest presence was still with me. In a Holiness Bible college! The people and I had not yet gotten the memo that the Lord was judging them as they judged me. Also, I did not get the memo about how the Holiness movement felt about Holy Spirit manifestations.

"Can you take a picture of those sheep that have strayed onto the college grounds?" the lecturer asked me in the middle of a lecture. I had gained a reputation in the college as a photographer. I ran to the shops to purchase a film roll (no smart phones yet) and ran back to the sheep.

I wanted to photograph the sheep with their faces toward the camera and the college building in the background. I went behind the sheep that were heading toward the college. This meant their backsides were facing the camera. I tried to call out to them to attract their attention, even for a moment, to get their faces toward the camera. No can do!

Who do you think strolled onto the grounds?

"Do want the sheep to face the camera?" the shepherd asked.

"Yes, please," I replied earnestly.

He mumbled some very strange sounds, and the sheep, as one, turned around to face the camera. I took several pictures, thanked the shepherd profusely, and rejoined the lecture. The lecturer used that picture in his sermons as he preached in various churches, promoting the Bible college. He commented that the enrolment at the Bible college had increased quite dramatically! It was a very vivid illustration of "the sheep follow him because they know his voice. A stranger they simply will not follow" (John 10:4–5). I will elaborate on the importance of hearing God's voice later.

BOSTON

"They will try to take it from you," the Lord said.

How absurd," I thought. *How can anyone take the Holy Spirit from a Christian, even from me?* I was about to go on a business trip to Boston with others from different companies. Having heard from the Lord, I was very uneasy, especially when we went for dinner together. Were they going to drug me and put me in a compromising situation?

Well, after dinner, I made it to the hotel room safely, or so I thought. Later, the Lord showed that, unbeknownst to me, I was drugged with Andriol at the restaurant. Andriol is a derivative of testosterone. I was also on steroids at that time. This potentiated the effects of the drug they put in my food.

Well, that night I wet my pyjamas. I was not going to sleep like that. I got up and washed my pyjamas in the bathroom. I had a feeling my room was also bugged. The news anchor in the morning amusingly said that there was a spill of oil from an overturned truck that had been cleared before the rush hour. "Behold," I declared to the Lord.

For the next four months, everywhere I went, people were playing games with me as if I had a guilty conscience. So this was their ploy to try to take the Holy Spirit from me. Then 9/11 happened. Some evangelicals in the US were talking of this as a judgment of God. I was thinking it was more like a slap on the wrist. The news anchors were careful to say it would take several months to clear the mess.

DEAL

The Lord was calling me to be a Jeremiah. "Lord I am not like that. I do not take pleasure in doom and gloom and judgment," I said.

"That is why I am calling you," the Lord replied.

I said, "Okay. But if you are going to call me to be a Jeremiah, I also want the gift of healing."

The Lord said, "Okay." He also said to extract the precious from the worthless (Jer. 15:19 NASB). This is why I state the works of other authors and the people who have taught me.

However, I realized by that point that a healing ministry was not likely to happen in a Holiness church. I did not receive this ministry for twenty years, when I joined Catch the Fire church and the Lord said, "Hang out with Pastor Steve Long for a while."

INCREASE

I prayed for the apprehension of those responsible for 9/11. Everyone was caught or killed except Osama bin Laden. I was constrained by the Lord not to pray for his apprehension yet. Years later, under the Obama administration, there were reports of a split in bin Laden's ranks. "Now command his apprehension," the Lord said. If the enemy is divided against itself, it cannot stand. I pointed my fingers like a pistol at a photo of bin Laden. Shortly after that, he was killed by the US Special Forces.

The Holy Spirit later revealed that in addition to trying to take the Holy Spirit from me, which was the first objective, they were trying to get me to give answers to some questions they had. This second storm period was the worst and the longest period I ever faced. And it was during the technology revolution. It was the second time I contemplated suicide. However, the groundswell of love that I felt sustained me. This was the eleventh time God saved my life. I also rejoiced in songs that glorified Jesus, which was what I wanted to see. These songs were honey to my soul and health to my bones. There were, and still are, many, many who love me even though there still are a very few malicious people.

Instead of having the Holy Spirit taken from me, I received an incredible increase in my authority and anointing. I will elaborate on this later. This authority was for interceding for the nations and events experiencing "God's slap on the wrist."

The Worship Songs

You Are Beautiful
Filling Up the Skies with Endless Praise
When You Walk Into the Room
King of My Heart
Chasing You
What a Powerful Name It Is
Great Are You Lord"
Oh My God There Is No One Like You
I Am a Child of God
We Love You, Can't Live Without You
I Love Your Presence
Our Affection, Our Devotion
Glorious You Are
You Lead Perfectly
We Pour Our Love on You
It's My Joy to Obey
All This for Your Glory
We Have Come to Give You Highest Praise
Here I Am to Worship

ACCUSATIONS

"One of the minors in the church is accusing your son of inappropriate touching," the pastor called to say. "And there is a witness," he continued. I was devastated. Interestingly, this happened after very meaningful prophesies for both of my sons. If the enemy cannot attack you, he will attack your children. After a police investigation, all charges were dropped, as the witness was found to have lied.

I urged my son to forgive all involved, and he has. When you are first charged, the police do target you and profile you, even if the charges are dropped. As it was, he was in trouble again with the law. There were mitigating circumstances, the charge was reduced, and he did not serve time. However, he is still facing the consequences in other ways. There was a third incident with the law, this time with both my sons involved. Again, the charges for both my sons were dropped. I took up the matter of the targeting and profiling of my son by the police with the Lord. Soon after, the police left my sons alone. These incidents were extremely draining on my wife and me, both emotionally and financially. We all, including both my sons, have forgiven all involved in these incidences.

While my son, who was lying on the sofa, and I were just chilling out in the family room, I asked him, "Do you know what my last name means?"

"No," he replied.

I said, "It means 'chief inspector of police.'"

He fairly flew off the sofa in utter surprise!

DID NOT GET THE MEMO

Again my food was adulterated. Again, malicious people were playing games with me, now for over ten years! Evidently they did not get the memo that God was judging them in the same way they were judging me. Manipulation, intimidation, setups, and even strong-arm tactics do not cut any ice with the Holy Spirit! In a last-ditch attempt, a plan was hatched to shame, humiliate, and ridicule me. But God. I just turned my face to the Lord, and the person hatching the plan himself was humiliated and ridiculed. I realized that he was not behind this and that he was instructed by malicious people. They tried to instruct him again, but this time he refused. The incidents and games only served to increase my anointing immeasurably.

Or do you think that I cannot appeal to My Father, and He will at once *put at my disposal* more than twelve legions of angels?
—Matthew 26:53 (NASB, emphasis mine)

CHAPTER 5

UNSPEAKABLE

I do not write this chapter to bring attention to myself. It is to say, "But God," when I was crucified and to make an important statement about spiritual principles that I learned from the Lord (when I was experiencing the storms), which I will delineate later. I know that during the events described below, many were praying as well.

NUMBER ONE

After the drought in England and subsequent deliverance, the Lord said, "I have given you authority over the elements because you interceded when I judged the nation." I later realized that the Jeremiah 1:5 calling was to intercede for a city or nation experiencing the heavy hand of God during the storms I was facing.

After the Boston incident, I implored the Lord for protection from the malicious people bent on trying to take the gift of the Holy Spirit from me. He spoke to me from Matthew 26:53 "Or do you think that I cannot appeal to My Father, and He will at once put at My disposal more than twelve legions of angels?" (NASB). Well, it wasn't twelve legions but six that the Lord granted. I was shocked! The Lord explained that He had not called the twelve legions so that I could.

"Lord," I said, "I do not have the wisdom or the knowledge for such authority or even how to command the angels, as I do not know the structure."

The Lord replied, "You shall command the angel in charge of the six legions."

"What is his name?" I asked.

To my utter shock, the Lord replied, "What do you want to call him?"

I thought for a minute and said, "Number One," based on a character in the series *Star Trek*.

The Lord said, "Okay. You will need to do prophetic symbolism of what I am going to do, and you will need to pray for them." I just had to command Number One accordingly.

9/11

"Abort the attack on the White House," I commanded.

The Lord had given me a vision of an imminent attack on the Twin Towers, the Pentagon, and the White House. My first thought was for the White House. Sure enough, the "let's roll" action resulted in the loss of the plane and passengers, but the White House was saved. Later, a book was published by the same title. The commands I gave were as directed by the Lord. Pointing my finger at the picture of Osama bin Laden was a command to Number One. Subsequently, I commanded that future terrorist attacks be thwarted. The US secretary of state traveled the world setting up a plan for just that. But the security forces needed to know where to listen and look. That's where Number One came in. He had the resources. There have been intermittent reports of the number of attacks that were thwarted and are still being thwarted. For obvious reasons, these are not generally released, but only as necessary.

TSUNAMI

"Protect the Christians," I cried out when I heard from the Lord about a huge tidal wave that would occur. On Boxing Day in December 2004, a tsunami hit the countries in the Indian Ocean. Later, I heard reports that an entire city was destroyed and only an elevator shaft was left standing. Most of the population was killed, but miraculously, the Christians survived. This led to the creation of a tsunami warning system.

SARS

"Command that there will be no new cases of SARS," the Lord said to me while I was on a business trip to the US. New cases continued to appear but at a reducing number. In two weeks, no new cases were reported in China, at least, where the outbreak was worst. Effective preventive measures were developed, and together with the development of a vaccine, SARS was eliminated. This was the beginning of the development of the flu vaccine, which has saved millions of lives since then. It is estimated that about three to five million flu cases occur every year globally, with 290,000 to 650,000 deaths. One year after SARS, there were an insignificant number of flu cases and no fatalities!

EBOLA

The Ebola crisis in Africa was going from bad to worse. Thousands died. The lack of a vaccine was compounded by the tradition of the nations affected in handling the dead. I figured the solution to this was a vaccine so that those handling the dead would not be affected. I commanded Number One to develop a vaccine in Canada, one that was at least 80 percent effective. He said he could make it 100 percent effective. I was so astonished! I said to do it. Soon after, a vaccine was developed in Canada that proved to be 100 percent effective. It was later mass-produced and distributed by the US.

ICELANDIC VOLCANO

"Behold," I said to the Lord. A few malicious passengers were playing games with me even while I was waiting at a boarding gate on a business trip. The flight experienced hailstones and storms. The passengers were petrified. You could hear a pin drop. I went to sleep soundly, confident that the small aircraft was not going to crash! However, soon after, the eruption of the Icelandic volcano caused the cancelation of more than 100,000 flights. For weeks. The smoke from the volcano covered the whole of Europe and spread toward Canada. I commanded that the smoke stop at the shores of Canada. It did!

FLOODS

The Germany floods of 2002 and the Calgary floods of 2013 will be in the memory of those affected for a lifetime. They were caused by very unusual weather patterns that required God's intervention to cease. Again, I was moved to intercede and command the storms to cease.

OTHER DISASTERS

And what shall I say about mad cow disease in the UK (three separate occurrences); the Hawaii volcano; the Japan earthquake, tsunami, and nuclear disaster; and diverse hurricanes and earthquakes? These geophysical events drew attention to global warming and the motivation for action on climate change. All of these also served to call people to prayer and to remind us that God is God and we are not and that God is not mocked. However, God works in all things to bring about good to those who love God, to those who are called according to His purpose. I have tried to show the silver linings mentioned in the events above.

The things which you have heard from me, in the presence of many witnesses, entrust these to faithful men who will be able to teach others also.

—2 Timothy 2:2 (NASB)

CHAPTER 6

---◆◇◈◇◆---

TRIAL CONDUCT

I cannot imagine I have been the only one (Christian or otherwise) who has experienced trials. "All who desire to live godly in Christ Jesus will be persecuted" (2 Tim.3:12 NASB). I share below some spiritual principles that are well-known but that in the heat of the moment or season of trial can either be forgotten or not put into practice. A wise pastor has said, "We are educated beyond our obedience." Put them into practice before the trials come, even the most elementary ones, and they will stand you in good stead. There are books galore on the milk and meat of God's word. In this chapter, I name some of the principles that stood me in good stead and some new ones I learned. The principles that follow are for situations of injustice, false accusations, persecution, hostility, etc. Other principles apply for healing, interceding for the unsaved, spiritual warfare, and the great tribulation.

HOUSE UPON A ROCK (MATT.7:24–25 NASB)

Building your life on the rock is of paramount importance. But simply coming to Christ is not going to cut it. The rock is the foundation. You have to build your house on it. How do we build our house on it? "Therefore everyone who hears these words of Mine and *acts* on them, may be compared to a wise man who built his house on the rock" (Matt.7:24 NASB). The Sermon on the Mount in Matthew chapters 5–7 detail the words that Jesus spoke about how we are to act. Acting on even the most elementary ones like "read the Bible and pray every day" will position you for obedience in bigger and bigger areas of your life. I was not a Christian and neither was my mother, but I walked in the little light that was given to me at age five up to age twenty-six when a blazing light was revealed to me.

But we need to act in faith, not only on the Sermon of the Mount, but also on words that the Lord gives us. Acting in faith means that if the Lord does not come through, we will fall flat on our faces by our actions. I describe some examples of acting on faith in my life in chapter 2.

BE ROOTED IN THE WORD

Without roots, of course the tree withers and dies. Roots are the means by which the tree draws its nourishment and water from the soil to grow. Our soil is the Word of God—the written, rhema, and kairos Word of God. If we do not feed on the milk of the Word when we first come to Christ (chapter 1, Begining), we will not be able to feed on the meat for sustenance to build our house (chapters 2, Growing in faith, and 3, Protection).

Being rooted is also important to have a history with God. The central history, of course, is that "if while we were enemies we were reconciled to God through the death of His Son, much more, having been reconciled, we shall be saved by His life" (Rom.5:10 NASB). Sometimes, in the heat of the trial, this is can be lost on us. We also need prior experiential deliverance of God in our lives to anchor our faith in trials. We need the Word and the Spirit. Several times the Israelites cried out to God for deliverance on the basis of what He had done before. (See Exod. 32:13; Deut. 7:18, 9:27, 32:7; Jud. 16:28; 1 Chron. 16:12; Neh. 4:14; Ps. 25:6, 42:6, 77:10; and many more.)

As you meditate on the Word and wait on God, He will give

you verses and promises to carry you through the trials. Some of the verses given to me were, "Cease striving and know that I am God" (Ps. 46:10 NASB); "The battle is the Lord's" (1 Sam.17:47 NASB); and "God causes all things to work together for good" (Rom.8:28 NASB). This means you need to be able to hear and recognize God's voice.

Hearing God's Voice

Hearing God's voice is extensively covered by Mark Virkler in his teaching on Habakkuk 2:1. Here I draw a note from how a child learns to recognize his or her parents' voices and learns language. Immediately upon birth, there is neural imprinting on the baby's brain that bonds the baby and mother. Also, even in the womb, the baby is constantly hearing the mother's voice and the voices of those around her. The spirit of the baby can also connect with the Holy Spirit if the mother is Christian. "When Elizabeth heard Mary's greeting, the baby leaped in her womb" (Luke 1:41 NASB).

By the time a baby is born, the child is already familiar with the noises he or she heard while developing in the womb, even worship songs. The child is immersed in a sea of words constantly every minute he or she is awake. As the child hears these words spoken, the pharynx is shaped to utter the sounds it hears. It is amazing how much easier it is for a child to learn a language than an adult. My spiritual father had six children, the parents spoke multiple languages, and the children grew up learning English, Hebrew, French, and German. Amazing!

If you spend your time in the presence of the Lord, reading the Bible, praying, and worshiping, you will likewise learn to recognize God's voice as the sheep recognized the shepherd's voice at the Bible college. The more clearly you recognize the real thing, the more easily you will recognize counterfeit voices. Just as the sheep recognized my voice as counterfeit when I called out to them.

PRAY AS PER PSALMS

I mentioned these psalms in chapter 4. However, when the psalms talk of the blessings on the upright, righteous, etc., pray for the Lord to help you to be upright, righteous, etc. When the psalmists talk of the misery of their enemies, pray that the Lord will forgive their enemies and bless them and that they will come to Christ, because of the misery the psalm mentions. After I prayed through these psalms several times during my trials, the Lord said I could just pray the first words of these psalms and that would be taken as me praying through the whole psalm. "My yoke is easy and My burden is light" (Matt.11:30 NASB). I will write more on this verse later.

DON'T DEFEND YOURSELF

The attacks on you are attacks on Jesus Christ. "The Lord knows how to rescue the godly from temptation" (2 Pet.2:9 NASB). You belong to God. You are bought with a price. It is His responsibility to defend you. Jesus did not defend Himself so He could defend you. When He was brought before the Sanhedrin, He could have kept silent and not answered them. They would not have had anything of which to accuse Him. And before Pilate, He could have spoken up in His defence and Pilate would have freed Him. But then how else would the scriptures be fulfilled?

FORGIVENESS

This is of paramount importance. The parable of the unforgiving servant in Matthew 18:21–35 makes this clear. This is extensively covered by John Arnott in his book *The Importance of Forgiveness* and by R. T. Kendall in his book *Total Forgiveness*. Here I will add the physiological basis of the importance of forgiveness.

Unforgivingness induces a fight–or–flight response that releases adrenaline. This releases sugars from the liver as a ready source of energy for fight-or-flight reaction when the sugars are used up. In unforgivingness, there is no fight-or-flight and the sugars are not used up. But they are not deposited back in the liver. They are deposited in the blood vessels, which are progressively blocked and are accompanied by serious illnesses. This was my experience described in the upcoming section "Do Not Fret." These in turn cause fear, anxiety, and stress, which cause other illnesses, infirmities, and conditions. But forgiveness leads to freedom from these as well as an increase in your authority and anointing as described below.

Do Not Rejoice

"Do not rejoice when your enemy falls, and do not let your heart be glad, when he stumbles" (Prov.24:17 NASB). It is not by your own hand that you have the victory, it is not even for your sake that the Lord gives you the victory, and it is certainly not for your glory. Professor Hallesby in his book *Prayer* shows that prayer therefore should be in His name, for His sake, and for His glory.

Instead of rejoicing, pray that the Lord will forgive them, even after the enemy has fallen, and for the Lord to restore and even bless them. If the Lord restores and blesses them, He will increase your authority and anointing immeasurably. This was my experience after I prayed for rain during the UK drought.

Delayed Answer

This does not necessarily mean no answer. When I was praying for rain during the UK drought, I expected that the Lord would send the rain during the meeting. That is why I took the umbrella with me. But during the meeting, there was no rain. I did not need the umbrella when I walked back home. But, as explained before, rain did come at a time when His name would be glorified best. Professor Hallesby elaborates this further in his book.

No Answer

When I went on the cruise, my prayers for the line to move in time for me to get into a taxi were not answered. The Lord showed me, as described previously, that He wanted to do exceedingly abundantly above all that I could ask or think. If there is no answer, this could be precisely the reason why, as professor Hallesby explains.

However, the reasons for delayed answer or no answer are not true for healing, physical or inner. This topic is covered in the chapter 7 on healing.

Honor Your Wife

"You husbands in the same way, live with your wives in an understanding way, as with someone weaker, since she is a woman; and show her honour as a fellow heir of the grace of life, so that your prayers will not be hindered" (1Pet.3:7 NASB). This is one of many reasons why some of our prayers are not answered. *Generally* speaking, God has equipped women uniquely with gifts that seldom operate in men. The most common is intuition. Our subconscious holds vast amounts of information that are not readily accessible by the conscious mind. Women are able to subconsciously access, process, and apply this information (without their realizing it) to their current situation. The resulting conclusion reveals itself as intuition. James Dobson chronicles several incidences of men's lives that were saved from disaster when they gave heed to their wives' intuition. So listen to your wives and do not be angry when they do or say things that do not make sense.

I have found this to be true in many instances when ministering in healing. On one occasion, a man's toe was not being healed. I asked him why he kicked something that caused the pain. He was angry with his wife. When we dealt with this and he undertook reconciliation with his wife, the pain went away, even before I prayed for him. On another occasion, a husband was healed partially but not 100 percent. When asked if there was something between him and his wife, he replied that he was mildly annoyed at her being the backseat driver. After dealing with this, he was completely healed.

TURN THE TABLES

The attacks of the enemy can be used as weapons against the enemy when ministering to others experiencing similar attacks. When you are attacked and are not delivered, pray for others you know who are experiencing similar attacks, but pray using the principle of divine exchange. For example, "Lord, I give this attack to you and leave it at the cross, and in exchange, I receive deliverance for my brother/sister in Christ who is experiencing similar attacks." When the brother/sister is delivered, you will receive deliverance as well.

I have found that this principle and that of hearing God's voice are important in the healing ministry as well. There are other principles in healing the Lord showed me, which I will describe in the next chapter.

DO NOT FRET

When going through the trials, I not only fretted but also harbored bitterness, rage, fear, anxiety, and stress. Bitterness and rage were the root causes of arthritis that I experienced as a result. After forgiving those involved, and the repentance and receiving of that forgiveness, the arthritis was healed. However, after a season, I became bitter and had rage again, and the arthritis returned. I again forgave, repented, and received healing. I experienced arthritis a third time. This time I was doubled over in pain. Although I forgave and repented, I did not receive healing. The Lord said, "For this you need others to pray for you." Vijeya, my wife, sent text massages to more than sixty saints. I soon recovered. I have not suffered from arthritis since then, well, not much. Fear, anxiety, and stress are root causes of eczema, which I also experienced. Again, I experienced deliverance after forgiveness and repentance.

Who pardons all your iniquities, who heals all your diseases.

—Psalm 103:3 (NASB)

CHAPTER 7

HEALING

DOUBTS

I have previously stated that God answers prayer in a way and at a time that will glorify His name best. However, this is not necessarily true of healing. But it must still be to glorify His name. The person receiving healing must still know it is Jesus Christ who healed. His desire is for healing. "I came that they may have life, and have it abundantly" (John 10:10 NASB). So why are not Christians healed routinely? It is not necessarily because Christians do not have faith that God can heal them. It is because of doubts. Will God heal me? Perhaps He is working on my character. Perhaps it is not the time for me to be healed. There are twelve doubts that Roger Sapp dismisses and refutes in his book *Without a Shadow of Doubt*.

These doubts stem from the experience of Job and Paul's thorn in the flesh (2 Cor.12:7). Job's problems were not from God but from Satan. So none of the "doubts" apply to Job. Paul's thorn in the flesh was persecution, not infirmity. The Greek word for thorn, *skolops*, is not used anywhere else in the New Testament but is used extensively in the Septuagint, which is the Old Testament translated into Greek. It is used in the context of persecution as in "the Philistines were a thorn in the flesh." When I realized this principle, the incidents of healings increased dramatically.

SOLUTIONS

So I declared to the Lord, "I know doubts are a block, but you are Lord God. How can I overcome doubts in people?"

He said something amazing: "I will heal scoliosis or any skeletal adjustments unconditionally, irrespective of doubts or any issues or factors, 100 percent of the time. When people see this, the doubts will go."

Wow!

Another way to remove doubts, I learned, is to ask the person if he or she is saved. If the person replies,"Yes," I ask if he or she is sure about that without a doubt. Naturally the person answers yes. I explain that the word *whole*—as in "as many as touched Him were made whole" (Mark 6:56 KJV)—and the word *salvation* have the same root word: *sozo*. So if the person has no doubts about his or her salvation, the person should not have any doubts about his or her healing. I then ask the person to receive Jesus as his or her healer as well as savior. Or I will say, "If Jesus were here, would you be healed?" The person always answers, "Yes." Well, then I will say, "Jesus is here. Be healed." And that person receives healing.

RESTORING THE FOUNDATIONS (RTF)

Doubts are not the only issue that can block our healing. Unforgivingness is huge in this respect and I described it earlier in chapter 6. Here I describe only some of the many issues that can block our healing. For a full treatment of this subject, I refer the reader to the very fine work of Chester and Betsy Kylstra on *Restoring the Foundations*.

There are a host of other factors that are instrumental in healing not being received. A few of these are bitterness, rage, fear, anxiety, and stress; fiery darts (negative words) of the wicked; generational sins and curses; ungodly beliefs; friction between female members of the family; and vows and pronouncements. These factors are extensively covered in the book called *A More Excellent Way* by Henry Wright and by the "Healing Rooms" model which extensively uses material from Wright's book.

Why is it important for these factors to be resolved? "Do not give the devil an opportunity" (Eph.4:27 NASB). The Greek word *topos*, meaning ground, is translated as "opportunity." If the legal ground for the demon to be there is not dealt with by the blood of the Lamb, "then it goes and takes along seven other spirits more evil than itself and they go in and live there; and the last state of that man becomes worse than the first" (Luke 11:26 NASB). This may explain why the Lord sometimes does not heal without the root causes being dealt with or when a person loses his or her healing.

"You have five minutes," the leader said at a meeting while I was on a missionary trip to India.

"What am I going to do in five minutes? I asked the Lord.

"Why don't you do what we talked about?" the Lord replied.

So I asked the people to stand up if they needed physical healing. Almost everyone of four hundred people stood up. I briefly commanded the healing for them. Only a few were healed. Then I led them through a prayer of repentance for the above listed issues and factors, and in forgiveness to those responsible for those emotions. Everyone was totally healed!

LISTENING TO GOD

So when ministering in healing, how do we discern which of the host of factors are operating? This is where listening to the voice of God is so important, as I described in the previous section. When I was ministering to a woman with a back problem, she mentioned that the Lord had told her to leave her job and take up employment where the Lord had directed her. The back problem was a result of the new work she was engaged in. So I just commanded (always in the name of Jesus) the healing so that she could continue doing what the Lord wanted her to do. She experienced very little healing. She returned the next week with the same problem. When she returned the third week, I finally asked the Lord, "Why is she not getting healed?" He replied, "You did not check with me!" I repented, asked for the reason, dealt with it, and she was healed. On the spot!

In fact, when I witnessed the very first healing, none of the factors I learned about were operating. I was on a ministry trip to England. The meeting was over, but people were still mingling and talking. I noticed a woman still in a receiving mode, and the Lord asked me to go speak to her. "What did you want the Lord to do for you?" I asked.

"I have back pain," she replied.

I asked if anything had happened before the back pain. She had been through a messy divorce some time ago, and she had experienced the pain since then. I asked if she had forgiven her husband, and she said she had. I was about to lead her to a forgiveness prayer for good measure, but the Lord stopped me. "If she says she has forgiven her husband, she has forgiven her husband," the Lord said.

So I waited to hear from Him. The Lord said to look at her feet. So I asked her to sit down and lift her legs a little above the floor so I could see if they were the same length. One leg was shorter than the other! The Lord asked me to ask the woman if she wanted the shorter leg longer or the longer leg shorter! She laughed and said, "shorter leg longer." I commanded this, and the leg grew to the same length as the longer one. When she stood up, I commanded the healing, and the pain disappeared except for some residual discomfort. The Lord said to command healing to all the areas where the demons were. She was totally healed. She was close to tears because the church had felt she was not being healed all these years because she had not completely forgiven her husband.

Be Aware of the Environment

After this meeting, I asked permission from my pastor to visit my parents. I narrated the miracle to my father, who remarked that he had one foot markedly shorter than the other. I replied that I was tired and would look at it in the morning. As I lay in bed that morning, I prayed, "Lord, I know this is a cultic environment and he is not a Christian, but heal him anyway."

Why would a cultic environment be a problem? When a blind man in Bethsaida was brought to Him, He "brought him out of the village" (Mark 8:23 NASB). After healing the man, Jesus said, "Do not even enter the village" (Mark 8:26 NASB). The unbelief of others around you does have an impact on the healing.

The next morning, I looked at his feet and said, "They are the same length."

He said, "During the night, I felt something in my feet."

Praise the Lord. But I noticed that the leg was bowed. I commanded the leg to be straight, and the bone actually straightened! He next asked for the lowering of his blood pressure, which was unresponsive to medications. His blood pressure was lowered too, as shown by the instrument that he had.

Putting these principles into effect saw the percentage of people being healed increase to 80 percent. Other factors not detailed in the works mentioned are described below.

Ungodly Beliefs

This is treated very well in *Restoring the Foundations,* but here I relate a story that illustrates a very important principle.

"Stand up if you need healing," the speaker at the conference said. I noticed one of the guests staying with my wife and I stand up. After ministering, the speaker asked those who were healed to sit down. A great many sat down, but not my guest. At the close, she still was not healed. The following morning, I asked if she was healed. She answered no. She was standing to receive healing for her backache. I offered to pray for her, to which she agreed. Still no healing.

I asked the Lord for the reason. "Ask her if she is saved," the Lord said. She said she was saved but that she wondered if God loved her. She repented of that, and she received healing.

I said, "Lord, there were a great many people who were healed at the conference without ministering to their issues. Why wasn't she healed there?"

The Lord said, "Sometimes people are healed under the sheer anointing, but if the issue is *with the character and nature of God, then that has to be resolved before prayer is answered*." Wow!

DIVINE EXCHANGE

But what if the factors involved are not known? Perhaps they stem from generations past, of which there is no knowledge. You may even be praying for someone unknown to you, at some distance away!

"Lord, I give the knee of my son to you and leave it at the cross, and in return I receive..."

"Stop," the Lord said.

I was about to ask for a completely healed knee in return as I had learned in *Restoring the Foundations*. I had been praying for my son's knee for some time but to no avail.

The Lord said, "Why don't you ask for the healing of the person paralyzed in the hospital?" The request for prayer was mentioned during the morning service from the platform. The Lord said, "He will be healed, and your son will also be healed."

I put this to the pastor, and he replied, "Are you saying he will walk out of the hospital?" I said yes. Two weeks later, we received word that the man walked out of the hospital! My son was also healed about a month later, albeit after surgery. We had been praying for this for some time as well, but we had failed even to get a surgery date. The wait-list was that long.

"By this all men will know that you are My disciples, if you have love for one another" (John 13:35 NASB). The word for love here is *agape* love. The same kind of divine love that Jesus has for His bride.

"As you sent Me into the world, I also have sent them into the world" (John 17:18 NASB).

"Bear one another's burdens and thereby fulfill the law of Christ" (Gal.6:2 NASB).

TAKE YOUR EYES OFF THE CONDITION

"But seeing the wind, he became frightened, and beginning to sink, he cried out, 'Lord save me!' Immediately Jesus stretched out His hand, and took hold of him, and said to him, 'You of little faith, why did you doubt?'" (Matt.14:30 NASB).

"Get the focus on the itching off them," the Lord said. I was ministering in healing on a mission trip to England. A child was brought to me with a skin itching condition. The father said the doctors had told him the itching should go away in a few weeks.

I replied, "Well, we do not want to wait that long." After I prayed, the Lord said to take their focus off the itching. *How am I going to do that?* I thought. Just then, Pastor Steve Long asked everyone to gather around to witness a miracle. *Well,* I thought, *that's how you do that.* After the service, the father said the itching had completely left.

Roger Sapp explains that Peter did not sink because he saw the waves or because he took his eyes off Jesus but that, because of these events, doubts entered. That's why Jesus said, "Why did you doubt?" When the father and daughter took their eyes off the itching, doubts had no opportunity to enter, and the daughter was healed.

BURDEN BEARING

"Can I use you for this ministry?" the Lord asked. I was reading John Sandford's *Healing the Wounded Spirit*, in which he explains burden bearing. This is when you experience the same condition that someone else is experiencing. When you get healed, the other person is also healed.

My wife was alarmed. My temperature was 104 F. There was no acetaminophen in the house. I had just finished a dose of antibiotics, and my temperature had been normal until that night. I drank copious amounts of ice water and put on layers of blankets and went to sleep. In the morning, I woke up soaking wet. My temperature was perfectly normal.

The doctor could not explain this. "The only condition I can think of is blood poisoning," she said. "This does not go away." Thankfully, blood cultures revealed this was not the case.

Later I realized this could be a case of burden bearing. I had forgotten the permission I gave the Lord. Later I learned that the daughter of one of the mothers in our church connect group who was receiving chemotherapy had suddenly developed a very high fever in the night (the same night I did) and the fever just as suddenly left!

FIERY DARTS OF THE WICKED (EPH. 6:16)

These are very real. One of the pastoral staff came to me with a sudden unbearable pain in the stomach. The Lord said it was the fiery darts of the wicked. I asked her if anyone had said some very negative words to her. She said that someone had. After we forgave the person, the Lord said to pull out the darts. I asked whether we should do it from the front or back. The Lord said from the front. I just grabbed the darts, in faith, and pulled them out one by one. She was instantly healed, apart from some residual effects. I commanded a complete healing of all the damaged areas where the demons were. No more residual effects. When ministering in this way, it is important to ask precisely how the darts should be removed, because we are dealing with demonic structures. It is so important to put on the whole armor of God at all times.

DEPRESSION

"Was it a big effort for you mentally to come here?" I asked. Depressed persons cannot receive the Word of God being proclaimed. They hear it, even believe it, but their condition prevents them from receiving it in their spirit. For this, they need a connection with the person ministering to them. This principle is explained fully in *Healing the Wounded Spirit* by John Sandford. That is why I asked the question. The woman connected with me. She knew I understood. Her ears were opened. I commanded the healing, and I could visibly see the depression lift and her expression change. Her face was beaming!

CONDITIONS ABOVE THE NECK

These conditions require a different approach. Call the spirit of the person to attention. Command the spirit to take from the Holy Spirit in the person (which means the person needs to come to Christ) and heal the condition. I can say that while applying this theology, I have seen glaucoma, dementia, and other mental conditions healed. This is treated very well by Arthur Burke but is outside the scope of this book.

DELIVERANCE FROM PORN, DIVORCE, AND ACCIDENTS

"I am struggling with porn and cannot seem to get victory over it," he said when I was ministering to him.

I was about to give a few scripture verses to him and bind the spirit, but the Lord stopped me and told me to ask him about his father. This was a generational curse. No sooner than we broke this,

his whole countenance changed, and he could actually feel clean and felt free!

I found the same to be true when ministering for physical healing for people injured in accidents and through divorce. When I point this out to couples with troubled marriages, there is such relief. They were pointing the finger at each other instead of at the enemy.

This shows the importance of listening to the Lord when ministering to people and not jumping to conclusions from past experiences.

FATHER'S CONVERSION

He had only days to live. I urged him to receive Christ. He said he saw his wife (who had passed away six months ago) very briefly. I knew this interaction with familiar spirits appearing as family members was a big stronghold in my parents' life. So I took a page out of Cindy Jacob's book *Possessing the Gates of the Enemy*.

Without moving my lips (as I did not want the enemy to know what I was praying), I prayed that the Lord would allow the familiar spirit to appear but to remove the cloak of my mother's appearance, leaving only the eyes. This would show clearly the true identity of what he was seeing. Sure enough, while I was with him in the hospital, he was startled out of his mind. I knew in my spirit that the Lord had answered my prayer, which only He could hear and the enemy could not. He apologized profusely to me for not believing me and accepted Christ. He died the following morning. However, I would not attempt this if you do not have a history with God!

A NOTE TO THE READER

This chapter is a synopsis of most of what I have learned in my healing ministry, both from others and from the Lord. If readers exercise the principles contained in this chapter, they will experience a greater degree of healing miracles in their ministries.

You shall not take a wife for yourself.

　　　　　　　　　—Jeremiah 16:2 (NASB)

CHAPTER 8

MARRIAGE

VIJEYA

She immigrated to Canada in 1981 and obtained her citizenship in 1985; both events are remarkable stories beyond the scope of this book. As a born again Christian, she joined a group reaching out to nominal Christians in Toronto. They formed close friendships that have lasted even to present day. Bruce and Doris Sinclair in this group played a pivotal role in our getting together.

They were missionaries in India and were now working at home base with Serving In Mission (SIM) responsible for the missionaries working in India. Unknown to Vijeya, Mrs. Sinclair sought to find a life partner for her. She asked a dear couple to forward their letter to a Sri Lankan pastor in England, asking if they knew of anyone suitable for Vijeya. However, the Sri Lankan pastor forwarded the letter to Ivan and Thelma Mark. This missionary couple was producing Christian radio programs in England for India with Radio Worldwide, a division of Worldwide Evangelization Crusade.

The Nudge

"Do you have a Bible at home?" I asked a couple passing me on a street corner in England where I was distributing tracts and Bibles.

"Yes, we do," they replied. "We are missionaries." Then they started to go their way. But they turned back to talk to me. They were Ivan and Thelma Mark. This was the beginning of a lifelong friendship until they passed away. Years later, I learned that Thelma had felt a nudge from the Lord to turn back and talk to me. Oh the importance of the Lord's kairos moments.

The Letter

"I have a letter to show you," Ivan said as we were talking one evening. It was the same letter that the Sinclairs had written. I promised to read it and go to the Lord with it.

Despite what the Lord spoke to me from Jeremiah 16:2 in 1975, I had told Him I wanted to get married. Hey, He is my heavenly daddy and I can talk to Him. He replied that I will have problems. I declared that He could take care of that.

"I am going to take you up on that," the Lord said.

"I want a Proverbs chapter 31 wife," I declared.

"Okay," the Lord replied.

Years later, I wondered if the Lord's Jeremiah 16:2 message to me was not a setup for my predictable reaction and expression of trust in the Lord.

The Peace

There were other conditions I placed on myself. I would not get married until I had known the girl for at least two years, and she had to be a Christian for at least as long as I was. However, when I read the letter about Vijeya, I was impressed by her devotion to God and her diligence in her responsibilities. I asked the Lord if this was the girl. He replied, "Let the peace of Christ rule in your heart" (Col.3:15 NASB).

So I put out a fleece to the Lord. I said to myself, "This is the girl the Lord has for me." There was peace in my heart. Then I said, "This is not the girl the Lord has for me." There was no peace in my heart. So that was that. I told Ivan that I would like to take this further. So much for my conditions!

THE SURPRISE

Vijeya knew nothing of any of this until the Sinclairs showed Ivan's letter to her. What spoke to her was that the Marks had already known me for six years, I was not ashamed of Jesus (I was witnessing), and the Word was important to me (I had left my job to go to Bible college for a year). It said to her that Jesus was important to me. The Sinclairs wrote directly to me. I wrote to Vijeya, and after her reply and more prayer, I wrote back and proposed to her. We got married in March 1985 in Scarborough, Ontario.

AWED

Reflecting on this, I was awed. A girl from Sri Lanka immigrates to Canada and becomes friends with the Sinclairs. After several years of getting to know Vijeya, they write a letter to a missionary that ends up with another missionary couple, the Marks. In the meantime, I meet the Marks in England after the fateful nudge and become friends with them for several years. And this is when the letter ends up with me. And I told the Lord I wanted to get married in 1975. He must have set the wheels in motion at that time!

MARRIED LIFE

Vijeya got up at 3:00 a.m. bawling her eyes out. I got up, startled. She explained that I left for work at 6:00 a.m., came home at 9:00 p.m., had dinner, watched the news, and went to bed. She did not have a chance to communicate with me. She was new to England, had no close friends or family nearby, and felt terribly lonely. It was during this time that she formed close bonds with the pastors John and Margaret Emms, who we had invited to Walt Disney World.

I was totally clueless to this new married life. Well, as I had done when I first became a Christian, I read books on the topic. Books by James Dobson, Gary Smalley, Stu Webber were very helpful.

As the Lord said, married life was not without its problems, which required a lot of resources. As the Lord said He would provide those resources. It was in the context of those problems that our love for each other grew. The principle of "love is decision" (Dr. James Dobson) is extremely important during the ups and downs of married life. Emotions come and go, which makes love very fickle as an emotion. You decide you are going to love someone. Period.

ADJUSTMENTS

"Have you been talking to my wife?" I asked one of the church members in England.

"How do you mean?" she asked.

"I said to you Vijeya is quite happy to go along with anything I say," I replied, "and you said I will have to talk to her."

She laughed. This was one of many adjustments I had to make in married life.

ADOPTION

"Where is the police report?" the judge asked at the adoption hearing in Sri Lanka.

Vijeya and I and all the parties there were devastated, floored, and panicked. We had spent several months diligently going through a lengthy adoption process. We had gone through a home study to determine suitability and obtained certified copies of all the necessary documents and had them authenticated by the Canadian government in Ottawa. Not to mention there was the process of finding Daniel as a newborn in Sri Lanka. How did we miss the police report?

"You have till next week to produce the report," the judge said.

Next week! Police reports had to be asked for in person in Canada! Thankfully, the Canadian embassy in Sri Lanka certified our documents for us to authorize Mr. Sinclair to obtain the police report on our behalf. He then traveled overnight to Ottawa for the authentication stamp and couriered them to us in Sri Lanka. We received the report just in time. Then came the lengthy process of Daniel's immigration to Canada. Birth certificates, passports, etc. had to be obtained. Three years later, we went through the whole process all over again for Joshua, armed this time with the police report as well.

The children had health challenges, which required a lot of resources. The Lord reminded me that marriage would not be a bed of roses but that I had expressed trust in Him. As faithful as ever, the Lord provided those resources.

"… in a moment, in the twinkling of an eye, at the last trumpet; for the trumpet will sound, and the dead will be raised imperishable, and we will be changed."

—1 Corinthians 15:52 (NASB)

CHAPTER 9

THE RAPTURE

INCREDULOUS

If you had told me in 1972 when I came to Christ that I would be writing about the rapture, I would have been incredulous, laughed, and dismissed the idea. If the great theologians could not agree on the subject, who was I? And that is still true. What follows in the next three chapters is mostly based on the work of Mikebickle.org on the person of Jesus Christ. As he has said, he is not into the end times; he is into Jesus Christ. So why am I writing about it? His work is voluminous, and I have endeavoured to organize and give a synopsis on the topic. There are many versions of the Bible, but only one Greek version. So I have looked at the meaning of the Greek words in the relevant passages and how they are used elsewhere in the Bible.

Part of my professional work is being an auditor. I question, investigate, research, cross-check, and do my homework. And I applied this process to Mike Bickle's work. I also listened to the Holy Spirit. So this chapter includes revelation by the Holy Spirit as well.

QUESTIONS, QUESTIONS, QUESTIONS

I wasn't even interested in the subject. Until 2012. I was reading an article by a pastor that declared Jesus would return in 2015. I told the Lord the Antichrist had not yet come to power. He asked, "What do you know about the day of the Lord?" He was not trying to put me down as if to say who was I to question it.

I replied, "The day of the Lord will come as a thief in the night." That was the extent of my eschatology!

"So you do not know when I will come again," the Lord replied.

The significance of that answer was not lost on me. If I knew when the Antichrist came to power, I would know the exact day Jesus would return. It would be 2,520 days later. If the day of His return cannot be known, then neither can the day of the Antichrist coming to power. The Antichrist would come to power and the church would not even know about it!

Obviously that article about the return in 2015 was off the mark, but only because the author jumped to conclusions. It was based on the blood moons of 2014 and 2015. "The sun shall be turned into darkness and the moon into blood before that great and notable day of the Lord come" (Acts 2:20 KJV). However, the verse does not say how long "before" is. And true to historical records, something terrible did happen in 2015: the war with ISIS.

Over the next several years, I continued asking the Lord questions, many but not all of which He answered. The Lord had to remove from me the prevailing and pervasive mindset on the rapture. The following is a summary of what I have learned from the Holy Spirit and from respected theologians.

CASE FOR PRE–TRIBULATION RAPTURE

Why would the Lord have the church go through the Great Tribulation? He rescued Lot and his family from the destruction of Sodom and Gomorrah, and He rescued Noah and his family from the great flood. He also rescued Israel from annihilation on three separate occasions. From the Egyptians when their backs were against the Red Sea, when Israel made a golden calf in the wilderness and Moses interceded for mercy, and during the time of Esther.

To further support this viewpoint, here are several scriptures:

- "Because you have kept the word of My perseverance, I also will keep you from the hour of testing, that hour which is about to come upon the whole world, to test those who dwell on the earth" (Rev.3:10 NASB).
- "These are the ones who come out of the great tribulation, and they have washed their robes and made them white in the blood of the lamb" (Rev.7:14 NASB).
- "And there will be a time of distress such as never occurred since there was a nation until that time; and at that time your people, everyone who is found written in the book will be rescued" (Dan. 12:1 NASB).
- "and you know what restrains him now, so that in his time he will be revealed. For the mystery of lawlessness is already at work; only he who now restrains will do so until he is taken out of the way. Then that lawless one will be revealed whom the Lord will slay with the breadth of His mouth and bring to an end by the appearance of His coming" (2 Thes.2:6–8 NASB).

The commonly accepted interpretation of this is that the Holy Spirit in the church restrains the Antichrist from being revealed until the Holy Spirit (and by implication, the saints) is taken out of the way (i.e., the saints are raptured).

CASE AGAINST PRE–TRIBULATION RAPTURE

With Sodom and Gomorrah, there was no righteous governmental authority. Lot and his family numbered only eight, and ten are required. That is why He removed Lot and his family before destroying the cities. With Noah, again, in the whole earth there was no righteous governmental authority. Noah and his family numbered only eight. Even when all the people on the whole earth were destroyed, Noah was not taken out of the world but was protected in the midst of the flood. During the tribulation, there will billions of Christians.

Again, the Jewish people were saved from annihilation by the Lord defeating the Egyptians and defeating their enemies during the time of Esther, not by removing them to a safe place.

The Greek word for "keep" in Revelation 3:10 ("I will keep you from the hour of testing") is *tereo*, which means to guard from loss by keeping the eye upon it. It is the same Greek word used in "I do not ask You to take them out of the world, but to *keep* [my italics] them from the evil one" (John 17:15 NASB). As well, the verse does not say to keep you from tribulation (Greek *thlipsis*) but from testing (Greek *peirasmos*). The term *tribulation* is used throughout the New Testament as in "In the world you have tribulation, but take courage; I have overcome the world" (John 16:33 NASB).

The Greek word for "out of" in Revelation 7:14 ("out of the great tribulation") is *ek ex*, denoting a point of origin. The point of origin of the great multitude is the tribulation. If they were raptured before the tribulation, that would not be their point of origin. It is the same Greek word that is used in *"out of* [my italics] Egypt I called My son"* (Matt.2:15 NASB).

The Hebrew word for "rescued" in Daniel 12:1 is *mawlat*, meaning "delivered" as in "to you they cried out and were *delivered"* [my italics] (Ps. 22:5 NASB). And "now there was found in it a poor wise man and he delivered the city by his wisdom" (Eccles.9:15 NASB). Nowhere is *mawlat* used in connection with deliverance by escape but rather in context of deliverance by the enemies being defeated.

Second Thessalonians 2:6 asserts that "you know what restrains him now." Why would they know about who restrains him more than two thousand years before the Antichrist is revealed? It is not the Antichrist that Paul is talking about being restrained. It is the spirit of the Antichrist (mystery of lawlessness) that is being restrained.

Restrained from what? Restrained from the lawlessness being expressed in the very embodiment of Satan (i.e., the full power of Satan expressed in a man). When this restraint is removed, then the Antichrist will be revealed. The Lord removes the restraint without the saints being removed.

We see the presence of the *saints* when the trumpets are blown in Revelation 8:3–4: "Another angel came and stood at the altar, holding a golden censor; and much incense was given to him, so that he might add it to the prayers of all the *saints* on the golden altar which was before the throne. And the smoke of the incense, with the prayers of the *saints*, went up before God out of the angel's hand" (NASB). We still see the presence of the *saints* when the fifth trumpet is blown in Revelation 9:4: "They were told not to hurt the grass of the earth, nor any green thing, nor any tree, but only the men who do not have the seal of God on their foreheads" (NASB). Which means there will be people who have the seal (i.e., the *saints*): "Who also sealed us" (2 Cor. 1:22 NASB).

The problem with the pre–tribulation thesis is that it requires a third coming of Jesus, a second coming with the rapture for the saints, and a third coming when He actually comes back with the saints to earth (Dr. Michael Brown in *Not Afraid of the Antichrist*).

Case for Post–tribulation Rapture

The question should be, "Why would the Lord keep the church from her hour of greatest victory?" Mikebickle.org. The saints will go through the tribulation but not experience it. The Greek word for tribulation is *thlipsis*. This is used all over the New Testament, including "in the world you have tribulation but take courage, I have overcome the world" (John 16:33 NASB).

However, the saints will be protected in the same way the Jewish people were protected during the plagues of Egypt:

- "But on that day I will set apart the land of Goshen, where my people are living, so that no swarms of flies will be there, in order that you may know that I, the Lord am in the midst of the land. I will put a division between My and your people" (Exod. 8:22–23 NASB).
- "All the livestock of Egypt died; but of the livestock of the sons of Israel, not one died" (Exod. 9:6 NASB).
- "There was thick darkness in all the land of Egypt for three days, ... but all the sons of Israel had light in their dwellings" (Exod. 10:22–23 NASB).
- "and when I see the blood I will pass over you, and no plague will befall you to destroy you when I strike the land of Egypt" (Exod. 12:13 NASB).

We see this protection also in Revelation 7:3: "do not harm the earth or the sea or the trees until we have sealed [Greek *sphragizo*] the bond servants of our God on their foreheads" (NASB). This passage speaks of the sealing of the 144,000 of Israel. However, the saints are already sealed with the Holy Spirit, "who also sealed [*sphragizo*] us" (2 Cor.1:22 NASB). Further, Revelation 9:4 states, "They were told that they should not hurt the grass of the earth, nor any green thing, nor any tree, but only the men who do not have the seal [*sphragis*] of God on their foreheads" (NASB).

This is not to say there won't be martyrs. And although there will be more martyrs than at any other time in history, the number will be small compared to the number of the saints as a whole. Persecution is what the Antichrist does to the saints, but tribulation is what the Lord (with the prayers of the saints) does to the Antichrist. Daniel 12:12 says, "how blessed is he who keeps waiting and attains to the 1,335 days" (NASB). The saints will be raptured at the last trumpet, 1,260 days, and will have resurrected bodies (1Cor.15:52). This is 1,260 days (three and a half years) after the abomination of desolation.

The people who attain to the 1,335 days are those who have not received the mark of the beast but are not Christians. These 1,335 days are the 1,260 days plus the thirty days travel by Jesus on a cloud around the world, and the forty-five days of travel on land to Jerusalem and setting up the world government infrastructure. However, these people who come to Christ when He returns will not have resurrected bodies, as they missed the rapture. When they die during the millennium, they will be resurrected with resurrected bodies. This is why Jesus said to Thomas, "Because you have seen Me, have you believed? Blessed are they who did not see, and yet believed" (John 20:29 NASB).

We see the presence of the Holy Spirit on earth even after the saints are raptured. "Seven thousand people were killed in the earthquake, and the rest were terrified and gave glory to the God of heaven" (Rev.11:13 NASB). This happens after the rapture of the saints at the seventh trumpet. "The rest" are those who did not receive the mark of the beast but were not Christians either. They resisted the Antichrist. The fact that they gave glory to God shows that the Holy Spirit was still present on the earth.

In fact, the Lord revealed to me that the pre–tribulation outcome would be the worst possible outcome. It is the prayers of the saints (and being received in the bowls) that releases the tribulation to defeat the Antichrist. If the saints were raptured before the tribulation, there would be no prayers and no tribulation, and the Antichrist will have the earth to himself without the Lord and the saints.

So I asked the Lord, "Why would you reveal the battle plan, as the enemy will know this as well."

He answered, "So that the saints will partner with me in the battle plan. But I have not revealed the day nor the hour of battle. The day of the Lord comes as a thief in the night," which means that each generation of Christians should live as if the Lord was coming in their generation! The next chapter gives a small snapshot of what this looks like, and it is based heavily on (apart from the study of Greek words) the superlative and voluminous works of Mike Bickle. There is good news: "His bride has made herself ready" (Rev.19:7 NASB).

Case Against Post–tribulation Rapture

There are more than 150 chapters in the Bible that deal with the period leading up to the Lord's return. Many of them deal with the invasions of Israel and Judah by Babylonians, Assyrians, Greeks, etc. How you view these chapters will determine whether the rapture is pre– or post–tribulation. A full discussion of these chapters is outside the scope of this book.

And while they were going away to make the purchase, the bridegroom came, and those who were ready went in with Him to the wedding feast; and the door was shut.

—Matthew 25:10 (NASB)

Write in a book what you see, and send it to the seven churches.

—Revelation 1:11 (NASB)

CHAPTER 10

PREPARATION

BUY OIL

Matthew chapter 25 is commonly thought to be about the Second Coming of Christ. That is not the case. The first word in the chapter is *then*. *Then* is Matthew chapter 24, which is about the generation of the Lord's coming (Mikebickle.org). So this is what Matthew chapter 25 is about. The virgins knew the Lord. "To Christ I may present you as a pure virgin" (2 Cor.11:2 NASB). They had ministries (lamps). But the lamps of the foolish virgins went out because they had no oil. They lost their ministries.

In the generation of the Lord's return, many will lose their ministries. The foolish got ready (trimmed their lamps) but had no authority (oil). They practiced piano and studied theology, preaching skills, and leadership skills, but they were empty. People will not want to know how big your ministry was or what great works you did. They will want to know if you can drive out the demon in their son when you visit. Many eminent prophets are prophesying a billion-soul harvest. This will require oil—authority of Jesus and fascination with God's beauty.

The foolish are not called evil. They may not lose their salvation. 1 Corinthians 3:15 says "If any man's work is burned up, he shall suffer loss; but he himself shall be saved" (NASB). However, if you cannot be faithful now, how will you be faithful during the great tribulation? Will you be pressured into receiving the mark of the beast? In that case, you will be reprobate, unable to repent, and lost forever. It is important to cultivate oil now. "Oil tenderizes the heart, enlarges our desires, illuminates our minds to spiritual truths, and produces a zeal for righteousness" (Mikebickle.org).

So how do we cultivate oil? Cultivating oil is cultivating intimacy with Jesus, in the secret place, in worship, in services where hosting the Holy Spirit is in their DNA. In other words, you cannot buy oil from others, only from the Lord. You cannot receive intimacy from others. It has to be your own. The wise could not give their oil to the foolish. "You have to engage in the God ordained process of acquiring intimacy. We have to get our oil by deep heart engagement with Bridegroom God, personal encounter and history with God to have authority that flows out of your spirit" (Mikebickle.org).

The four parables in Matthew chapters 24 and 25 and Luke chapter 21 show the importance of responding to His leadership.

In the parable of the fig tree, we are commanded to watch the biblical signs unfold to grow in understanding and prayer. It is an exhortation to grow in strength in our hearts.

In the parable of the unfaithful servant, we are told to be diligent in the face of pressure and disappointment. This parable shows that the Lord's coming is sooner than you think.

The parable of the ten virgins shows the importance of cultivating intimacy with Bridegroom God. Here, the delay in His coming is longer than you think.

In the parable of the talents, we are to be faithful even in small ministries. Delay is harder than you think. Most Christians do not have big ministries, but collectively they have a big ministry.

The most important admonition, in Matthew chapter 24, to empower us to cultivate oil in these ways is to "watch and pray." This is mentioned twenty times in the New Testament, nine times by Jesus, and once by Paul. If communities and saints watch and pray, then they will have resources and answers. Watching gives wisdom, and prayer releases God's power to escape being caught in a snare during the tribulation. If we watch and pray, we will make godly decisions.

Do Not Compromise

The letters to the churches mainly admonish against compromise, except for Smyrna and Philadelphia. They did not need this admonishing. Emperor worship was prevalent and intended to ensure loyalty from the emperor's subjects. Christians were put to death as criminals. As well, wealthy guilds (trade unions) required members to attend worship feasts for the god Apollo. These feasts involved immorality, sorcery, and covetousness which is idolatry (Col. 3:5). Refusal to participate would result in people losing their employment. "Immorality stimulates the body outside of God's will, sorcery stimulates the spirit outside of God's will and covetousness puts confidence in money instead of the Lord" (Mikebicke.org).

Do not lose your first love as admonished to the letter to Ephesus. Ephesus was the financial center and capital city of the Roman province of Asia Minor, hosting the temple of Diana. This combined religion and sexual immorality. Silversmiths prospered because of the sale of silver and bronze idols. After becoming Christians, they burned these. The silversmiths' trade dried up. No wonder they stirred up the authorities.

The church was the largest and most influential since the church in Jerusalem was scattered in 70 AD. However, the church lost its first love. They were told to repent and return to their first love or He would remove their lamp stand out of its place (Rev.2:4).

Do not be lukewarm. If you are cold, you will be aware of your condition and more open to repentance. If you are lukewarm, you are not aware of your condition (i.e., you do not love God with all your heart). Do not hold to the doctrine of Balaam or the Nicolaitians, who perverted the freedom and grace in Jesus Christ and, on this basis, allowed participation in pagan feasts.

ETERNAL REWARDS

There are more than fifty references to Jesus' teaching on rewards: Romans 14:10–12; 2 Corinthians 5:10; 1 Corinthians 3:8–15; Romans 5:17; Matthew 25:21; Revelation 3:18; Matthew 6:20; Colossians 3:1–2 are a few. The eternal rewards of faithfulness will blow your mind. They go far beyond our salvation.

> Jesus said "he who receives you receives Me, and he who receives Me receives Him who sent me. He who receives a prophet in the name of a prophet shall receive a prophet's reward ... And whoever in the name of a disciple gives to one of these little ones even a cup of cold water to drink, truly I say to you, he shall not lose his reward." (Matt.10:40–42 NASB)

Just receiving a prophet results in a prophet's reward. The Greek word for receive is the same in these verses. It means to believe in and receive what Jesus or the prophet has to say, not just hospitality. Believing is not just head knowledge but heart knowledge. Belief needs to result in action. It means receiving Jesus brings the same reward as Jesus has! We get to minister with Him, wage spiritual warfare with Him, ride into battle with Him, and reign with Him!

The talents parable shows generous rewards. Both the servants with two and five received the same affirmation: "good and faithful." Good because they had godly motivations and faithful because of diligence in face of problems, pressures, and obstacles. They were willing to sacrifice comfort, honor, and personal agendas. Most have a small assignment, but it still matters because collectively it is huge.

Ruling with Jesus is related to faithfulness. Saints will have great joy ruling in partnership with Jesus. The smallest effort is not forgotten by God and is written in the book of remembrance before Him (Mal.3:16). Those who have spiritual understanding, inspiration, and tender hearted responsiveness to God will grow in knowing God. More will be given to them. They will have an increased awareness of grace to be ruler over much.

The rewards for faithfulness mentioned to the seven churches are phenomenal. Of course, not all the rewards are given to all the saints. Saints will have power over the nations (Rev.2:26–28). They will be given the hidden manna that speaks of increased revelation of Jesus and the morning star, which is a deeper relationship with Him. The white stone is the invitation to the wedding banquet. When a host arranged a banquet, he would send the guests a white stone, which was their wedding invitation. On the stone was written what the guest means to the host. The saints will receive a white stone with a name written that no one knows except Jesus and the guest! Those who are invited to the banquet get to ride with Him at Armageddon (Rev 19:8, 14, 15).

They will get the crown of life. This is not just salvation. The Greek word for life (*dzo-ay*) is the same as the one used in the following verses. The implications of the crown of life are unbelievable!

- "I am the way the Truth and the life" (John 14:6 NASB).
- "He who believes has eternal life" (John 6:47 NASB).
- "Tree of life" (Rev.2:7, 22:2 NASB).
- "Book of life" (Rev.3:5 NASB).
- "River of the water of life" (Rev.22:1 NASB).

The Greek word for physical life is *psoo-khay*as in "sought the Child's life" (Matt.2:20 NASB). Crown signifies ruler and authority. We are talking about the crown of life as implicated in the above verses.

Saints get to eat of the tree of life. Again, this is not just salvation, as they are already saved. It is eating of the very new revelations of Jesus and Father God and Holy Spirit. Ultimately, it is dining with Him at the marriage supper of the Lamb. Overcomers receive authority over the nations and the morning star. Saints will be pillars (authority) in the temple of God, and He will write on them the name of His God and the name of the city of His God, the new Jerusalem, which comes down out of heaven from His God, and my new name! These names are eternal remembrances of your service to God. Saints are granted to sit down with Jesus on His throne!

Saints will receive white linen garments. These are not just the garments of salvation and robes of righteousness, which all believers receive. These are garments that are worn denoting righteous acts of the saints (e.g., at the marriage supper of the Lamb)(Rev.19:8). Their names will not be blotted from the book of life.

These rewards should encourage believers to be faithful during the tribulation and not be intimidated into receiving the mark of the beast. It is easy to say that saints love Jesus for who He is, not for the rewards. But the saints will be blown away by unexpected and very generous rewards.

Micah 7:5–20

CHAPTER 11

————— · ❈ · —————

THE END

Whether the rapture is pre–tribulation or post tribulation, it is best to err on the side of caution. What if the church does go through the tribulation? What should Christians do in that environment? To understand this, we need to get an idea of what that environment looks like.

SOCIETY AND CULTURE IN THE GREAT TRIBULATION

The period of the great tribulation is more than the seals, trumpets, and bowls. It is also about the prevailing culture and society of that day. "Do not trust in a neighbor; do not have confidence in a friend. From her who lies in your bosom guard your lips. For son treats father contemptuously, daughter rises up against her mother, daughter-in-law against her mother-in-law; a man's enemies are the men of his own household" (Mic.7:5–6 NASB). Micah writes about the conditions in his day, but Jesus relates it to the end times. "You will be brought before rulers and kings for my sake … The gospel must first be preached to all the nations … brother will betray brother … children will rise up against parents and cause them to be put to death … when you see the abomination of desolation flee …" (Mark 13:9–14 NKJV).

This society is already operating in Western China. There are cameras every hundred yards to an estimated total of 600 million! These are linked to each other and to facial recognition and artificial intelligence. This system can track anyone from the time they leave their house.

Everyone receives a starting social credit of three hundred according to several reports. This score increases for acts of kindness, public volunteer service, pro government actions and statements, etc. As the score increases, they get increased privileges and benefits, job promotions, etc. This score also decreases for criminal acts, unsocial or criminal behavior, and especially for attending Christian services or gatherings. This results in loss of privileges, loans denied, demotions, or even job losses and denial of accommodation.

However, it doesn't stop there. If someone with a high social credit score does not betray a friend, family member, or acquaintance who they know is a Christian (who will have a low score), then that person's high score is reduced to the same as that of the Christian! They are forced to betray them.

During the period of the tribulation, all the governments of all the nations will be united in their opposition to the Christian faith (Ps. 2:1–3). It is not beyond imagination that they will use this kind of technology in their persecution of Christians. At the time of writing, the UK started implementing the facial recognition camera system!

CHRISTIAN LIFE DURING THE TRIBULATION

The principles outlined in chapter 6 ("Trial Conduct") will be of paramount importance, particularly that of "turning the tables." The principle of divine exchange in Chapter 7 ("Healing") will be very important.

The theology of divine exchange can also be applied to other areas apart from healing. I tried this with career opportunities for someone in the church, and she received a very lucrative opportunity, albeit a temporary one. But this proved to be a stepping-stone for continued lucrative opportunities. A job was also obtained for the person I was praying for, for some time. And my wife also got a job.

I experienced several setbacks after I was laid off. The Lord was showing me that I could give these to Him and receive success for others. I could leave my hopes, dreams, and even the prophesies that I have received at the foot of the cross and receive in turn the same for other saints. I will also receive the same in turn.

However, I feel that the Lord was showing me that the full measure of this will be realized when all saints enter the same type of intercession. If they give their disappointments, sicknesses, infirmities, losses of inheritance, periods of unemployment, and even prodigals to Him and ask for answers for other members, then they will also receive their answers. "By this all will know that you are My disciples, if you have love [*agape*] for one another" (John 13:35 NKJV). "Bear one another's burdens and so fulfill the law of Christ" (Gal. 6:2 NASB). The Greek word for bear is *bastazo*, meaning to remove or lift. "As you sent Me into the world, I also have sent them into the world" (John 17:18 NASB).

Micah chapter 7 details seven responses to the Lord during these times:

1. I will wait expectantly for the Lord; I will wait for the God of my salvation (Mic. 7:7 NASB). Jesus admonished His people to "watch and pray." Look at this time as an opportunity by leaving your situation at the foot of the cross and receiving from the Lord increased authority and anointing. Look to the Lord, not to your enemies and what they are doing.

2. "Though I fall, I will rise; though I dwell in darkness, the Lord is light for me" (Mic. 7:8 NASB). This is not a time to be overcome by failure. It is a time to get back up. It is time to trust in the Lord's leadership, in His promises, in what He did for you at the cross. "For a righteous man falls seven times and rises again" (Prov. 24:16 NASB).

3. "I will bear the indignation of the Lord because I have sinned against Him, until He pleads my case and executes justice

for me ... I will see His righteousness" (Mic. 7:9 NASB). While going through this process, we cannot quit our divine assignment. The sin may not be of the flesh but also of the spirit (i.e., unforgivingness, bitterness, rage, complaining, etc.). This process leads to greater love, humility, generosity, and gratitude.

4. Take responsibility. "I have sinned." (Mic 7:9 NASB). Do not blame others or the culture or intimidation or pressures, etc.

5. "Shepherd your people ... as in the days when you came out of the land of Egypt, I will show you miracles. The nations shall see, ... and come trembling ... to the Lord our God" (Mic. 7:14–17 NASB). Intercede to the Lord during this time. Several approaches to intercession are described in chapter 6 ("Trial Conduct"). The Lord promises deliverance, as when He delivered Israel from the Egyptians (Exod. 7–12; Rev 7:3; 9:4).

6. "Who is a God like you, who pardons iniquity ... because He delights in unchanging love" (Mic. 7:18 NASB). This is a call to worship God in awe and adoration for salvation so great, so full, and so free.

7. "He will again have compassion on us" (Mic. 7:19 NASB). We are to show mercy to others as He has shown mercy to us. Saints cannot be at odds against each other or even with non-Christians if they have not received the mark of the beast. If forgiveness is important now, it will be of paramount importance if the saints find themselves going through the tribulation. "For judgment will be merciless to one who has shown no mercy; mercy triumphs over judgement" (James 2:13 NASB).

For God so loved the world, that He gave His only begotten son, that whoever believes in Him shall not perish, but have eternal life.

—John 3:16 (NASB)

Therefore they said to Him, "What shall we do, so that we may work the works of God?" Jesus answered and said to them, "This is the work of God, that you believe in Him whom He has sent.

—John 6:28–29 (NASB)

EPILOGUE

LOVE

"Dad, Jake has darted out through the door!" the son yelled frantically. It was a stormy night, and Jake was his beloved pet dog.

"Don't worry. He will return," the father reassured his son.

An hour passed, but no Jake. "I am going to look for him," the son exclaimed.

"No," the father said. "You stay here. I'll go and look for him."

However, after a long time, the father returned with no Jake. The son was adamant that he wanted to go look for Jake. Finally, the father agreed to go with his son.

Soon the son heard a whimper above the noise of the storm. "That's Jake!" the son yelled excitedly.

Jake had fallen into a ditch and had been unable to climb out again. Returning home with Jake, the son asked the father, "Why did you not hear Jake crying?"

The father replied, "I don't know, son. Maybe you love Jake far more than I."

God loves you far more than you can ever think, and even your least insignificant sigh does not escape His attention!

OVERPAYMENT

This is a scene from an Indian movie.

"How much do you want for that office tower?" the Indian businessman asked.

Bracing for negotiations, the seller quoted an exorbitant price to start. To his surprise, the businessman replied, "I'll pay it!"

After shaking hands on the deal, the seller remarked, "You are not a good businessman. If you had bargained with me, I would have reduced the price."

"My mother brought me up as a single mother," the man replied. "She worked her fingers to the bone day and night on that building to put me through business school. I am now a successful businessman. I am buying it for her. You are not a good businessman," he told the seller. "If you had asked for more, I would have gladly given it!"

Jesus Christ paid the biggest overpayment in history for you (Sermon by Duncan Smith).

GOOD KING WENCESLAS

Good King Wenceslas actually existed and was known for his benevolent acts, especially toward the poor. The carol was written two hundred years after his death. So he was something of a legend in this respect. When he saw the poor man gathering winter fuel, he could have sent his servants or soldiers to deliver the provisions (from the king's table)! But he did not. He chose to leave his comfy castle and deliver the provisions himself, with his page, through the "rude wind's wild lament and the bitter weather." That was sacrificial of the king. When the peasant opened the door, he got to dine with the king (in his own house)!

God could have just commanded our salvation. He could have just said, "John be saved", or "Mary be saved." Instead, He chose to leave His home in heaven, die a shameful death on the cross for you, and bring you the provisions from the King's own table. All you have to do is open the door of your heart to Him. "You prepare a table before me in the presence of my enemies" (Ps. 23:5 NASB).

ECCLESIASTES

Solomon lived a life of splendor, majesty, fame, and fortune. But he was also an extraordinary achiever. His book chronicles all of this. Yet he concludes, "Fear God, and keep His commandments: for this is the whole duty of man" (Eccles.12:13 KJV). We were made for God. We cannot find satisfaction in putting ourselves to anything apart from God. We did not bring anything into this world, and we cannot take anything from this world. Or can we? The question throughout ages—why—cannot be answered apart from Him. Why am I here on earth? Good question. Thought you'd never ask.

However, as generations since Adam have discovered, it is not possible to obey God in our sinful nature anymore than it is possible for an orange tree to produce apples. Our nature has to change. How? By coming to Jesus Christ. His death on the cross atoned for our sins that separated us from God. When that happens, the Holy Spirit will come into your heart, change your nature, and become an enabler for you to live a Christian life.

Does that mean that when a person comes to Christ, he or she is sinless and perfect? Not by a long shot. But in God the Father's eyes, he or she is. However, the next step is also important: to be baptized in water and with the Holy Spirit. There is something very powerful in declaring yourself to be a follower of Christ at baptism. It declares to the heavenly realms and to others on earth that you belong to Christ. This starts the process of God shaping you into a chosen vessel to glorify His name. You begin to understand why you are on this earth.

So can we take anything from this world with us? You bet! Jesus says, "But store up for yourselves treasures in heaven, where neither moth or rust destroys, and where thieves do not break in or steal"

(Matt.6:20 NASB). Chapter 10 ("Preparation") describes the mind-blowing rewards for faithfulness even in little things.

So you start by coming to Christ with this simple prayer:

> Dear Father God, I know I am a sinner but that Jesus Christ died for me on the cross for my sins. I repent of my sins and take Jesus Christ to be my Lord and Savior. I ask Jesus to come into my life and heart. Baptize me with the Holy Spirit for Him to enable me to live a Christian life. Order my steps so that your will be done and your name be glorified. In Jesus Christ's name I pray, for His sake and glory. Amen.

If you have said this prayer, you need to be connected to other believers in a spirit-filled church or contact me, the author of this book. And be prepared for a ride of your life!